You know that the purpose of college is to provide you with a good education, but you may not realize that more is learned outside of the classroom than inside. Your total college experience can be both profitable and enjoyable, but by no means will it be easy. **How to Survive and Thrive in College** provides a help for those times when the going gets rough and all hope is lost. But this book is more than just a survival manual. It shows the student how to thrive and mature at college. As a college professor with strong Christian convictions, Dr. Cliff Schimmels presents a practical and insightful guide for all college students, and for those considering a college education.

HOW TO SURVIVE
AND THRIVE IN
COLLEGE

BY Cliff Schimmels

How to Help Your Child Survive and Thrive
in Public School

HOW TO SURVIVE AND THRIVE IN COLLEGE

Cliff Schimmels

Fleming H. Revell Company
Old Tappan, New Jersey

Library of Congress Cataloging in Publication Data

Schimmels, Cliff.
  How to survive and thrive in college.

  1. College student orientation—Handbooks, manuals,
etc. 2. Study, Method of—Handbooks, manuals, etc.
I. Title.
LB2343.3.S34 1983   378'.198   82-20409
ISBN 0-8007-5104-3

Contents

Part III
THE INSTITUTION

Preface

I have a great job. I teach college seniors.

Some of them are even in their last semester—they just finish my course and waltz right into the commencement line.

Since mine is the final course in a teacher preparation program, these students will become certified teachers. Within three months many of them will step into their very own classrooms in an elementary or secondary school somewhere.

Now think about that for a moment. For several of these people, their time has come. Some of them set these professional goals as much as a decade ago. (I said *decade* instead of ten years because it sounds longer.) For years, they have had that one dream—that one big goal. They wanted to be teachers. With great anticipation, they hurried through high school; and for the past four years they have been hurdling the obstacles of college (some pretty big leaps) and learning as much as they can so that they can get the license and knowledge to teach. And now they are almost there.

I like to teach people at this stage of their development. They are a little nervous—caught in the paradox of being "hyper" and exhausted at the same time. But they are eager, and they are happy. They can see the goal. They can see the end, or rather they can see the end that will lead to the beginning—the beginning of that magic life of doing what they always wanted to do.

I always go to graduation exercises. I wouldn't miss them for anything. During the years when my raise in salary doesn't keep pace with the cost-of-living increase, it's the most rewarding day of the year. On this day I remember why I became a college teacher.

After the exercises, I stand around outside and wait to congratulate the graduates. Since I am one of the last obstacles they had to hurdle (I may not be tall, but I *am* big around), most of them still remember me. I get lots of hugs, and I even get a kiss once in a while. When you're middle-aged, forty pounds overweight, and balding, that isn't bad pay for a semester's work.

As you read the rest of this book, keep that scene in mind—those screaming, happy graduates, throwing their hats in the air, waving their diplomas, posing for pictures with all their friends of the last four years, greeting their parents, and hugging their professors.

I want you to keep that scene in mind as you read this book because it is this happy scene I had in my mind while I wrote it. I have actually been accused of writing a sad book. In fact, some of those very seniors I have been talking about took issue with even the title.

"Don't use the word *survive* in the title," they told me. "College is a much better experience than survival. The word is too negative. Say something positive."

But of course those were the words of people who were not only survivors but thrivers. And besides, I think I *am* saying something positive.

Whatever your reasons for beginning a college education, they are sufficient to lead you on to finish it. Don't be deceived. During the process, there will come times when you won't be so sure. There will come times when you will doubt yourself and your ability. There will come times when it would be easier to chuck all plans, along with that half-finished term paper and those unread one thousand pages of history, into the proverbial wastebasket and spend the rest of your life busing tables at the ski lodge. There will come times when you will lose sight of the reasons you had for starting, and when you do that, you are in trouble.

That is when I want you to remember those happy graduation

scenes. I have seen the last act so often that I am convinced it is worth living through the entire drama to get there. And that is what makes this a happy book. I have given you the final scene first, so you know how it is going to turn out. You can tell right away that this is going to be a happy story. It ends with a joyous celebration.

So as you read the book, especially the first chapter on setting the stage, keep reminding yourself of that happy final scene. If you allow it to, this is all going to work out. Don't forget those new graduates. And besides, I will be waiting in the reception line to get my hug from you.

HOW TO SURVIVE
AND THRIVE IN
COLLEGE

1

Setting the Stage
or
How to Sleep on a Damp Pillowcase
(And this is a *happy* book?)

College! That word was magic to you even before you grew tired of high school. And why not! You know that college stands for excitement and intellectual stimulation and freedom. After all, you have seen enough Saturday afternoon football games on TV to know all about college life—bundling up and going to the football game with the gang, sitting in the card section, playing in the band on national TV, caring for the live monkey mascot, wearing preppy clothes and dating a preppy person.

Of course, you realize that all that is just the fun part, but you know about intellectually stimulating study too. You have seen those commercials where the students working in white coats in the lab discover a new cure for a plant disease, and you have heard your older friends in college talk about their classes with such pleasure that they have everything nicknamed. College people take classes in things like "Psyke" and "Sosh" and "Polly Sye" and "Bio"—classes that deal with the significant problems of the world and even help you understand your own self. With titles like that, they have to be exciting. Now that is something to look forward to.

So based on this knowledge of college life you have put together from several sources, you begin to grow impatient with high school. Even your best friends are beginning to wear on your nervous system with their constant childish pranks. You resent those mandatory classes in history, math, and science, and you dream of the time when you can major in something really stimulating, like psychology or sociology or anthropology. You watch your high school teachers' sincere efforts to deal with the material, but you know that if they were really bright, they wouldn't be doing this. They would be teaching college somewhere. You observe the curfew of 11:00 on weeknights and 12:00 on weekends which your parents set, but you say to yourself, *Just wait. When I get to college, they won't even know.*

Like the Christmases you waited for when you were younger, the day finally comes—the day when you pack all your clothes and records and say good-bye to home and hometown. Oh, there is a tinge of a feeling of transition when you brush your teeth that morning and realize that your toothbrush will never belong on that particular peg in that particular bathroom again. But there is too much to look forward to for you to dwell on such feelings for very long. You'll never get to college if you don't leave home sometime. Everybody knows that. So anticipation takes over your thoughts once more.

When you get to the campus, you face another minor crisis. You would really like to show your parents around, but your desire to get into this romantic thing called college life wins out. So you say your good-byes in front of the dorm, and with baggage in hand, you confidently strike out into the unknown future.

After waiting in line at the dormitory registration desk for about thirty minutes and correcting a slight mix-up about the size of your advance deposit check, you get a key of your own, a laundry-assembled package of clean linen, and directions to room 318.

You take the stairs instead of the elevator because you want to suck in all the nuances of the place, and as you wander down the hall slowly searching, you almost suffer from sense overload. You are working so hard at distinguishing and cataloging every sight, sound, odor, and taste that you almost reach the point where your sensing mechanism just shuts itself off.

Finally, you find it—room 318. From the slightly ajar door, you assume that there is someone inside already. So with years of accumulated expectation and anticipation, you fling open the door and come face to face with a strangely strange and yet strangely familiar person. It looks like someone you might have known from high school, but it isn't. This person is a stranger—a total stranger—someone you have never seen before, someone about whom you know absolutely nothing. And yet, this is the person with whom you will share your life for the next several months. You will study with him in the room; you will sleep with him looking on; you will ask his opinion about what tie to wear when you go out on dates. In short, you will undress in front of this person—physically, emotionally, and perhaps even spiritually.

He sticks out his hand and says, "Hi. I'm Roger Your Roommate. It looks like we will be living together." (This is written from the male perspective for no reason. The feelings here are universal; they aren't the special domain of either sex. If you are a girl, you've just met Rosanna Your Roommate. Only the names have been changed.)

Now, stop and reflect for a moment. Are you ready for this occasion? Are you ready for the give-and-take necessary to establish a living relationship with someone who has not lived at your house? How are you two going to get acquainted? How are you going to work out your differences in body schedules, musical interests, and study needs? (And don't be deceived, there will be differences.) Will this stranger be able to take the place of all your family and friends?

But enough of this. We can't dwell here too long. College is too exciting to waste time on thoughts like those. You must get on with this business of being a college student.

You begin the process of moving in, staking your claim to the parts of that fifteen-foot square which will be home for you. You take the bed on the right because Roger already has claimed the one on the left. You choose the desk facing the wall because Roger has his books stacked neatly on the one facing the window, and you tell yourself that you can always put up a poster if you get bored. Since Roger has his clothes already in place, you choose the closet that last year's inmates forgot to clean. In other words, you establish yourself in places that Roger has left for you, and you don't even remember how you used to decorate your own room.

As you stack and store, you and Roger begin the process of getting acquainted, of establishing one of those lifelong, college roommate friendships that you have always dreamed about. Because there is no other common ground, you naturally talk of high school days. You played football; Roger was captain. You finished in the top 10 percent of your class; Roger was salutatorian. You were in Key Club; Roger was president. You were in the church youth group; Roger sang a solo part in the *Messiah*. As this one-upmanship continues, you feel a big, hollow pain take root and grow in the bottom of your stomach. (Actually, if you are fortunate enough to escape this conversation with your roommate, don't gloat. There are plenty of people around who will be very pleased to make you feel humble about your accomplishments. You will meet most of them during the first few days you are on campus.)

And from this positive beginning, the roommate relationship grows until two days later, you and Roomie walk to the dining hall, stand in the ubiquitous line for a quarter of an hour, eat your meal, and walk back to the dorm together without saying one word to each other. When you think about it later, you are astounded to realize that you are only mildly astounded.

But there are more people at the college, so you begin to broaden the friendship base. You meet the other people in the dorm, and with those guys you begin to learn what college is all about. In the best of academic tradition, you grease doorknobs, make mock telephone calls to unsuspecting victims, hide each other's underwear, plot against the people who came to college to study, and stage pillow fights. (Of course, you may not actually engage in any of the above categories; they are only examples. *Your* pranks, regardless of how creative and sophisticated you may think they are, will seem just as childish to the assistant dean who is appointed to worry about such things.)

Occasionally, in the midst of all this fun, you get the feeling that you really shouldn't be doing some of these things, and frequently when you sense that someone is really upset, you wish you hadn't gone so far. But there is a sense of achievement to all this. At least, you are part of the gang.

Meeting the opposite sex is another matter that requires diligent planning. The techniques can range all the way from yelling out the dormitory window to the more civilized method of attending the freshman mixer, staged by the upperclassmen who have been assigned the task of keeping the freshmen within the boundaries of human behavior.

At the mixer, you spot her. She may not be *the one,* but at least she will do until you get yourself better established. The next night, you take her to the first fifty-cent flick of the year (something filmed in 1932), and on the way back to the dorm you decide to see what the football stadium looks like after dark. You soon discover that your date has more sophisticated expectations. The possibilities frighten you, so you decide to sit on the dating urge until you either build up your confidence or find someone as naive as you are.

But enough of this partying and social life. Classes start. That is the inevitable rule of college. I have been around these institutions of higher education every fall for the past twenty-six years; and every year, to nearly everyone's surprise, classes start. Be ready. The same thing will happen to you. Oh, by this time, you might even be quite an accomplished college student, depending on whether fortune has chosen to smile on you. You might have been the one whose medical examination was lost in the registration procedure and who had to stand in line for three days before it was finally found, tucked away in a file at the assistant dean's office. Or you might have been one of the lucky ones who chose the science class that required $73.29 worth of books. Or you might have been one of the many whose registration form and schedule were rejected by the faultless computer and who couldn't find a human with the authority to kick or kick against the machine.

Nevertheless, classes start for even those people. Although you are not ready, you probably have worn yourself rather thin by now, and you appreciate the opportunity to sit down and put the old brain to work for a few hours every day. Besides, you have exciting classes.

The first is psychology—one of your favorites in high school—and you can't wait. You go in early, find a good seat, put your books away so they won't hinder you, and prepare yourself for a good discussion. About seven minutes after the class was to start, the professor, who looks even younger than your high school teachers, enters the room, marches to the podium, opens a notebook, and begins to read in a monotone. By the time you realize that he is serious, you have already missed the major points in the outline, so you get out your pen and notebook and start writing frantically. But the lecture isn't too well organized; he uses gigantic words and alludes to people you've never heard of. You look around with your "misery loves company" glance, and you see your classmates writing away with an air that says they understand every word. Suddenly, you find yourself hating these people whom you've never seen before, and you especially hate that guy standing at that podium, talking too fast about things you can't comprehend.

When class is over, you try to reorganize your jumbled notes, but they are too scrambled, so you go to the Union and play a game of pool instead.

Why *not* play? No one is putting any pressure on you to study. You have not had one clearly defined assignment since classes started. And since your notes aren't making all that much sense anyway, you begin to ask serious questions about the value of even going to class. So you don't, once in a while. After a particular card session that lasts too long into the night, you sleep in the next day and try to forget about that 8:00 A.M. psychology class where all you do is sit and work on your project of making a square with an *X* in it and hips on each side without lifting your pencil. Anyway, you have four years to master that feat. What is one day? Actually, you find that skipping class is a bit like getting olives out of a bottle: after the first one, the rest come rather easily.

After you have been in school about seven weeks and are just getting concerned about whether your team can win the intramural flag football championship, the professors all throw you a curve. On Wednesday, you go to your classes and every prof says the same thing: "We'll take our midterm exam this Friday. It will count for about a third of your semester grade. Actually, this will be just a short quiz, covering the first 1,400 pages of your text, all the class notes, and the twenty-six outside readings that were assigned on the syllabus." Suddenly, flag football doesn't seem all that important.

Since this is already Wednesday, you take a quick glance at an hour-by-hour schedule and realize you can't do it. You just can't read all those pages and organize all those notes. But you must try. Your parents are depending on you; your high school friends are depending on you; somehow you get the feeling that the whole world is looking over your shoulder to see how you do on those exams, question by question.

It is now that you learn the meaning of a new word: *the all-nighter.* In fact, you learn it so well that you slip in two in a row—three hours' sleep in two days. The backs of your eyeballs smart. The telephone rings and you are too tired to answer it. You wear the same socks three days in a row because it would take too much time and energy to wash out a clean pair. And right in the midst of all this, Roger comes in and in his sweetest tone asks, "Can I borrow your tennis balls?" You forget all you ever learned about the sin of hate.

Although you remember a speech you once made in high school about foolish housewives who get addicted to over-the-counter uppers, you take the "no-sleep pills" when the guy down the hall offers you some. There are times when coffee and Coke are just not strong enough. And you study—through the night and through the next day.

Glassy eyed and numb, you take the exams, but you know the results even before you hand in the answer sheets. There are simply too many things you haven't even heard about.

When the results are posted the next week, your fears are confirmed—two D's, an F, and a C. Not only have you never had grades this low in your life, you have never known people with grades this low. (The two D's, an F, and a C are but illustrations. Regardless of what you make, the grades will probably be much lower than you ever expected when you said good-bye to your parents many weeks ago.)

At this point, if you are normal, you will probably do some real soul searching. Your roommate relationship (or some other close relationship) is not as satisfying as you had wanted it to be. You have pulled pranks that went against your sense of good taste. You have practiced moves on dates which have made you feel a bit unclean. The college has fouled up your account. The classes have been stale and slow, rather than exciting and stimulating. You have listened to so many bizarre ideas spoken with authority that you have grown callous, and you rarely notice anymore. Your grades brand you as a dismal failure. You have never been so tired in your life. You miss your parents, and you still have eight weeks to go before this nightmare comes to an end.

Don't be surprised if your pillowcase turns damp during the night. Somehow you missed this moment when you were learning about college from those Saturday afternoon football games.

Dedication

It is to that very night that I dedicate this happy book. Remember the opening illustration—all those happy graduates celebrating their success. Believe it or not, they probably all went through the "Night of the Damp Pillowcase" at least once and maybe more often. It is fairly common. But it is this moment that is crucial. This is the moment when one decides whether or not he wants to become a happy graduate, whether he wants to get up, dry his eyes, dust off his books, organize his notes, and get on with the business of surviving and thriving in this enterprise called college. *It can be done.* If you got in, you can finish; and every graduation day, I am again convinced that it is worth finishing.

Every commencement I realize that these graduates have not simply finished an ordeal. They have done much more than that. They have grown intellectually. They have expanded their minds, their interests, their friendships, their abilities, their talents, and their curiosity.

They have not only prepared themselves for a profession; they have also prepared themselves to live their lives with a new perspective and a new meaning.

The rewards of a college education go deep and last throughout a lifetime. They are worth the effort.

For those of you who need some help, I offer the advice in this book. I know it is sound because I have gathered it not only from personal experience, but also, more recently, from those college seniors who will soon be celebrating the victory of having survived. I have interviewed more than three hundred of these people, and I have put together the most common and most insightful of their points. Perhaps the most interesting thing I found in my research is that the advice these students of the 1980s gave would have been appropriate to the college students of my generation more than a quarter of a century ago. I think we can conclude that the techniques for surviving and thriving in college are universal. If one piece of this book doesn't fit your particular situation, read on. The next piece might save you some spots on your pillowcase. (I also might add that although this opening illustration was written from the male point of view, this book is relevant to the female students. In fact, most of my counselors on the project were female.)

So if you are a beginner looking at the possibilities of investing four years in a college education or if you are presently a student at one of those "Night of the Damp Pillowcase" points, I hope this book can supply you with some encouragement as well as some practical, helpful hints so that you can not only look forward to graduation, but enjoy the process of getting there as well. And if you have already survived the process, perhaps the book can provoke some pleasant memories.

Organization

At first glance, the organization of the chapters might appear to be a bit absurd, but there is some logic to it. I hope it will be as apparent to you at the conclusion as it is to me. I have tried to present the chapters in the order they were listed in the opening illustration.

I have chosen to deal with the social scene first because that is not only the first part of college life you will encounter, it is also the most important. If you are going to thrive, as well as survive in college, you must learn to manage a variety of social experiences; and when the college career is over, those lessons and friendships will probably outlast the lessons of books and classes.

The second section of the book offers specific suggestions for playing your way through the academic scene. Most of these generate from common sense. In fact, probably everyone who ever went through college could read these chapters and say, "Why, I know that." But most of us knew these things better after we had finished than before we started. So I am going to give you an edge. I am going to give you the practical hints which some people must learn through tough experience. If, as you read this section, you will realize that I am trying to make things easier for you rather than tougher, you just might have some time to play tennis during midterm week.

Finally, in the last section on the institutional scene, I talk about some of the personal problems you will encounter as you relate to the institution of college—choosing a college, picking a major, and dealing with the bureaucracy.

Theme

There is one final word of warning before you begin reading the specific chapters. All the suggestions in this book are predicated on the assumption that before you begin college life, you will have made a thorough study of one particular part of your anatomy—your *fingertips.*

I'm serious. Think about it for a moment. Study those fingertips and think about all the ways they can help you through the college experience. You can use them to poke on the typewriter when you beat out that twenty-five-page term paper the night before it's due. You can use them to plug up your ears when the noise in the dorm gets unbearable. You can use them to flirt with the person who sits across from you in psychology class.

But if you look more closely, you will discover that your fingertips have a more important function than all of those above.

Look, for a few seconds, at that diagram etched on the ends of your own fingers. There are more than 5 billion people on this earth right now, and not another one of them has that particular diagram printed on the tips of his fingers. That is your diagram—your very own pattern. The Creator, omniscient and omnipotent, did a very special work when He put you together, and the proof is as close as the tips of your fingers.

When the world closes in on you, when classes seem unbearable, when your friends make unusual demands, when your grades fall below your expectations, don't forget the message at the end of your fingers. That Artist who drew your pattern is willing and able to help you be who you are if you will let Him.

I hope this book encourages you to remember the lesson of your fingerprints throughout your college experience. The most important tool for surviving and thriving in college is a healthy self-concept—an objective view of who you are and what you are capable of contributing to the world.

You must not lose sight of that, and to help you remember, God put a symbol of your uniqueness at the end of your fingers.

Part I

THE SOCIAL ACTIVITIES

2

Roommates

"Fish and visitors smell in three days"—Ben Franklin.

Most experiences in college are just variations of experiences you have had before. Attending a college class is more like going to class than anything else. The teaching style may be a little different; the class may be a little bigger; the words may be a little longer; but the rules are the same as in high school; and the desks are just as uncomfortable.

Whether you are in junior high or graduate school, studying is the process of putting your face in a book and keeping it there until someone's data and ideas become familiar enough for you to repeat on a test.

Whether you are sixteen or sixty, dating consists of boy asks girl, girl accepts, they go, boy pays, and if they have a good time, they repeat the procedure. College dating is just a variation of that ancient and accepted plot.

By the same reasoning, making friends is a personal art that doesn't change much between the ages of eighteen and eighty.

Living Together

Most of college life is just adapting familiar situations to a new setting. The one difference is the business of living. If you are typical, the biggest difference between college and high school is that you live at college. Probably for the first time in your life, you will live away from home; and whether you live in a sorority or fraternity, a dorm, an apartment, Aunt Hilda's Rooming House, or the local Holiday Inn, you will probably live *with* somebody. Adapting to this situation is the first and the most crucial adjustment you will have to make if you are going to survive and thrive in college.

I realize that this advice may be falling on deaf ears. You know all about college roommates. You've seen the movies. You've heard the stories of the sacrifices roommates make for each other, of the lifelong friendships that come from a chance meeting when two people are thrown together as freshmen. You have looked forward to the joy and sharing and good times—to having the "twin" you've always wanted.

Well, I hope it works that way for you. It does for some—for a very few; but for most, adjusting to a roommate, any roommate, is a tedious, humbling activity which demands some frustration, some thought, and some maturing. It is probably the single most significant educational experience of your whole college career, but as is often the case in learning, gain frequently comes from pain.

However, the pain usually pays off. Most roommate situations work out, and in many cases, roommates do become closest friends. That is why I offer this advice. I want your relationship to be one of the happy ones.

Culture Shock

What actually happens when you move in with someone else is that two distinct and diverse cultures are merged. Your family is one culture with its own mores and taboos. Some of these you have already identified. You know the ritual for birthdays and Christmas and new driver's licenses, and you know how these are different from similar rituals in the homes of your friends. In fact, you are probably rather happy about those differences.

But those major differences are representative of a whole list of things which distinguish your background culture from that of your roommate. How you squeeze the toothpaste tube, how you gargle, how you wake up in the morning, the sequence in which you dress yourself, how you take care of a book, and your idiomatic expressions are all part of your distinct culture.

When you move in with a roommate, the two of you will have to adjust to each other's strange habits. This may seem like a fun challenge to you, and it probably will be—for three days. But when the newness wears off and you settle down to the routine of living, those little cultural differences can become downright irritating. After you have just stayed up until 3:00 A.M. to study for a midterm exam, your roommate's 6:00 A.M. gargling noises can constitute a declaration of war.

Since this is such an important point to your success in college, let me illustrate. I cannot stand to hear someone chew ice. For me that sound ranks right up there with scraping the fingernails down the chalkboard as the most hideous noise in the world. In my culture, chewing ice is a violation of human decency.

Since I am emperor and king at my house, no one chews ice in my culture. I don't have to live with that sound when I am within the boundaries of my own castle.

If you and I were college roommates, you couldn't chew ice. If you did, one of us would have to leave or we would fight. Those are the only two options. There is no way for me to overcome my cultural bias. (And before you label me as an inflexible old man, let me tell you about my friend who can't bear to watch someone sit with his foot curled under him.)

Regardless of how suited you and your roommate are to each other, you will still have to adjust to the cultural differences. How you do that is a personal matter depending on what kind of people you are and what kind of adjustments have to be made. But it wouldn't hurt you to think about it. Adjusting to your roommate is a necessary and educational part of college life. You should look forward to the challenge, but with some reservation.

Advice to the Novice

I do have some suggestions. When I interviewed those three hundred college seniors in preparation for this book, most of them gave at least one specific and emphatic suggestion for promoting harmony in the room. Let me list some of them.

- Always live with your best friend.
- Never live with a friend, but live with someone you hardly know or care to know.
- Always ask before you borrow.
- Never borrow from your roommate.
- Live with someone who has the same major as you, so the two of you can study together.
- Never study in your room, but find a place in the library from the very start.
- Honor your roommate's individual rights in the room.
- Demand your rights as an individual. After all, you have paid for half the room.

So what do we gather from this list of contradictions? Just what I said at the beginning: Merging two cultures into a working relationship within the confines of a fifteen-foot-square dorm room is a personal matter. It can be done, but you are going to have to work at it.

Two Tests

The first place to start is to know yourself. That may sound like a strange request that smacks of some way-out, mystical philosophy. But I am serious. Before you go to college, stop and take stock of yourself. Know what is important. Know what is absolutely important and what is only semi-important. Know what makes you a nice person and what makes you a nuisance. Even if you don't want to admit this to someone else, at least be honest with yourself.

The second point for you to devote some attention to in this matter of the roommate relationship is the art of communication. I have never seen a good relationship between two people without good communication. In fact, I suspect that almost every flaw that exists in a relationship can be traced to a weakness in communication between the two. I don't want to beat a cliché here, but I do want to make a point. You and your roommate need to talk. There are no shortcuts. You need to be as honest with each other as you were to yourself in the paragraph just above. You and your roommate may even become lifelong friends. That possibility depends on how much you respect him and how well you communicate with him.

If you have trouble in the communication department and it is hampering the relationship, let me suggest a test—a simple paper-and-pencil test that will get at some of your cultural differences. (This isn't original with me. I stole the idea from those magazines dedicated to saving marriages.)

A Compatibility Test for You and Your Roommate
(Fill it out separately, then share answers.)

1. Are you a late-night or early-morning person? During what part of the day do you function best? (Place yourself on the continuum.)

   Early morning _____ late night

2. How do you wake up in the morning? (Place yourself on the continuum.)

   Don't say a word to me _____ Hi! What a nice day!

3. What are your three most dreaded pet peeves? List them in order.

   a. _____

   b. _____

   c. _____

4. Name two habits you have which you think would annoy someone else. (These could be personal. You talk to yourself, scratch, belch, brush your hair compulsively, or brag. This is honesty time, and there is no need to try to hide it. Your roommate will find out eventually.)

   a. _____

   b. _____

5. Do you like silence or noise when you study? _____

6. What is the most important thing for you to get out of college? Rank the following one through six.

   _____ Grades (so you can get to graduate school)

   _____ Friends

   _____ A spouse

   _____ Memories (A whole catalog of good times for you to tell your grandchildren.)

   _____ Yourself (A discovery of your own individuality and worth.)

   _____ A degree

7. What is your favorite kind of music, and what kind of music can you simply not stand?

   Favorite _____

   Rejected _____

8. Do you hold grudges or forgive? _____

9. What do you do when you're angry, yell or keep coldly silent? _____

10. Do you like to make decisions or do you like to follow? ____

11. Are you organized or do you prefer to do things spontaneously? _____

12. Do you like the room clean or cluttered? Place yourself on the continuum.

    Clean _____ Windstruck

   This is only a suggested list. You can add or delete as you wish. Actually, the questions themselves are not as important as the activity. Through a process like this, you and your roommate may discover the art of communicating with each other; and if you do, you are on the road to a happier college experience.

Human Rights

Once you and your roommate have learned how to talk to each other, you need to discover what you have to give up and what you can't give up in order to live with each other.

Without sounding like one of the founding fathers of our country, I submit that there are certain inalienable (I've never known what that word means) human rights, and every living situation must provide some opportunity for the exercise of these rights. For the purpose of brevity and clarity, I categorize these rights into four classes: the right to individuality, the right to privacy, the right to property, and the right to companionship.

1. The right to individuality. You are a unique human being. The tips of your fingers prove that. As a human being, you have a right to be yourself. Of course, you can't infringe on other people's rights, but at the same time, you need to come face to face with the reality of being yourself, of being who you are without pretentions or apologies. You can put on a false face some of the time, but you have to take it off once in a while. When you are in college, the place to do this is in your own room.

If you are a very secure person with a positive self-image that won't be damaged through four years of college, you won't have any trouble with this. But if you aren't, you need to take measures to guarantee that you can achieve some degree of individuality in your room.

There are two areas where this is particularly important—your vulnerability and your devotions.

As a human being, you have faults—everybody does. You have some flaw in your physical or emotional or intellectual makeup that you would just as soon not expose. Like the soft spot in the baby's head, it's there. So far, you have been very selective about whom you have let see that flaw. But now, you will probably have to show it to your roommate. Can you trust him or her enough to be vulnerable?

Your devotional life is also a very private matter. Of course, there are times when it is appropriate to share your faith. In fact, you are commanded to do so. But your faith originates in an inner shrine where you communicate with your Creator. You have an inalienable right to enter that shrine by yourself, and that's your devotional life. You shouldn't have to surrender it just because your roommate may not understand what you are doing.

2. The right to privacy. When you have daydreamed about going to college, you probably haven't dreamed about private times. When I daydream, I always picture social times with me as the center of attention. But every human has a need to be alone occasionally. (If for nothing else just to discover whether he likes himself and can stand his own company.) It may be hard to get those times in college. When you share a tiny room with one person and a bathroom with fifteen people, you may have to work at getting some time for yourself.

I suggest that roommates recognize this need within each other and honor it. It may be as simple as asking your roommate to step out of the room for ten minutes. Or perhaps the two of you could develop a signal system that says, "Don't come in right now. I want to be alone." Or you could schedule times during the day when the room belongs to one person. Of course, this privilege can't be abused by either one of you, but you do need to respect the other's need for privacy.

3. The right to property. You may be the world's most unselfish human being, but you still have a need to sense that something is your own personal possession. Because of the closeness of a dorm room, it is quite easy for two people to lose sight of property boundaries. Frequently, "mine" has a way of becoming "ours." And soon, the two don't know who owns what. Toiletries, cosmetics, books, clothes, records, and so on run the risk of becoming community property, and more often than not, this will lead to a problem. How severe the problem depends on the people involved, but I suspect there is always a problem. Somebody will feel as if he is being cheated.

My suggestion is to keep the property boundaries intact from the start. This will eliminate hard feelings later. In Shakespeare's play *Hamlet* Polonious sent his son Laertes off to college with this reminder, "Neither a borrower, nor a lender be." That is still good advice.

This property issue also relates to space. It seems to me that every American is entitled to a certain amount of space that is his very own. My wife sleeps on the left side of our bed. That is her space; and even though her light is better than mine, when I lie in bed to read, I would never think of lying on her side.

Honor your roommate's possessions and his space.

4. *The right to companionship.* Now that I have suggested that your college living situation provide you with room for your individuality, your privacy, and your sense of property, let me contradict all this selfishness by suggesting you also need some companionship.

In the next chapter, I will talk in detail about college friendships—about where they come from and what they are good for. But here let me say simply that your roommate is a worthy candidate to provide you with support and encouragement. After all, he has seen you in your underwear and he knows where your soft spot is.

If you and your roommate have different interests and activities, you may need to work at developing this companionship. I know some roommates who have built an effective relationship by reserving a specific time each week to spend together. Every Saturday morning they get up and go to breakfast, or they go out to eat on Thursdays, or they play tennis every Sunday afternoon.

The time and activity isn't important. What is important is their need to develop a sense of companionship.

The Upbeat

Lest I have overstated my case and frightened you about your prospects, let me assure you that thousands of roommates make the adjustments and live together quite comfortably and perhaps even joyously. If they can do it, so can you.

In fact, sometimes it even turns out positively.

A few years ago, I applied for a job that I thought would allow the full exercise of my talent. After filling out all the preliminary material, I went through what I felt to be a very successful interview. The director and I seemed to be able to communicate. I felt confident that I could do the work and have a good time doing it. I had all the necessary skills, and I could be loyal to the company.

I didn't get the job. The director gave it to a college roommate he had twenty-five years ago.

3

Friends

"Our family always takes its vacation the last two weeks of July. We've been doing it for years. We get together with three other families from around the country—one from Texas, one from New York, and one from Florida—and we all go to Wisconsin for camping and fishing. They're all old college buddies of mine. We've just stayed close through the years."

* * *

"Our daughter is engaged now. Her fiancé is the son of an old college friend of mine. The kids met several years ago when we went out to visit them."

* * *

"Just got back from my twenty-fifth class reunion. It was sure good to see all the guys again. About fifteen of us went to this all-night restaurant, and we stayed up and talked until 3:30 A.M. What a great bunch of guys."

* * *

"I'm flying out to California tomorrow. I'm a casket bearer at a funeral of an old college friend."

* * *

"My one regret about my undergraduate days is that as a pre-med major, I just didn't have the time to get as close to some of the people as I would have liked."

* * *

I cite this list of direct quotations, all of which I have heard in the past twelve months, to set the tone and the theme of this chapter on college friends. The friends you make at college could easily become the most significant and most permanent acquisitions you obtain during those four years.

I don't want to discredit classwork. That's how I make my living! But at the same time, I am aware, sometimes acutely aware, of the value of the friendship-making procedure during the college experience. I am aware that many of you will remember your friends much longer than you will remember your classes and those golden gems that fall from the professors' mouths. I am aware that the times you spend horsing around in the dorms or frat houses, going to games, planning and executing the perfect practical joke, lounging in the lounge, or playing pool in the Union are good times. You don't need to be ashamed of them or embarrassed by them. Those could be among the best times you have in college. But on the other hand, those could be the very times that doom you, both as a student and as a person. Friends are an integral and valuable part of the college experience; but like any good thing, they can become too much. Friendships have to be monitored with wisdom and discretion. That's why I put this chapter second in the book—ahead of the section on how to do well in the classes.

You've made friends before. You may be better at it than I am, so you probably don't need a too-obvious explanation of the process. You will make college friends much like you've always made friends; and when it's over, you (if you ever think about it) will be fascinated by the circumstances, events, and pure luck that led you to the people you are close to. We will probably never understand why we like certain people or have developed a relationship with them. I don't want to rob you of that risk and romance in the friendship-making process. But since college friends can be both permanent and devastating and are such a significant part of the total experience, you need to think objectively about this whole aspect of college life before you make certain decisions or fall into certain situations inadvertently. Perhaps I can provide you with some tools for that objective thinking.

Roles

In every human relationship, there is a dominant figure and a recessive one—a leader and a follower. Every time I say that I get yelled at, but I say it anyway. Being yelled at is a small price to pay for being right.

The yellers always say, "But you don't know the kind of relationship I have with my good friend, Cathy. We are equals. Share and share alike. We are mutual partners."

I don't agree. If that were true, the friendship would never get anywhere. There are thousands of subtle decisions which have to be made, and someone in the relationship must assume the responsibility for making them. I am not talking about gigantic affairs, but the simple, everyday decisions of procedure. When you eat out, you may choose a restaurant by mutual agreement; but who decides which table you occupy, whether you turn right or left, who sits in the booth and who sits in the chair, when do you stop conversation and have the blessing?

I suspect that if you will examine every relationship you have, you will discover what I am saying. With some of your friends you are the dominant force. (Does that sound like something out of *Star Wars*?) With others you are recessive. With some, you are quite comfortable making the decisions. With others, you are more comfortable letting them make the decisions. The awkward moments come when you are just getting acquainted with someone, and the two of you have not yet discovered your appropriate roles.

I am in the process of breaking in a new boss, a new department chairman. Although he is my boss, I am more talkative than he. Because of my respect for the man and his position, I wanted him to be the dominant person in the relationship. But because of our personalities, I tend to dominate. After having been together for five months, we have both discovered how to function within our appropriate roles, but we had some awkward moments while we were learning this.

From this discussion about these roles, I would like to convince you of three points. First, you need a variety of friendships so that you can fill both roles. You need some friends with whom you are the leader and some with whom you are the follower. Next, it is important for you to know what role you fill in a specific relationship. If you are the leader, you may find yourself in the position of assuming responsibility for the outcome of the friendship; or, if you are the follower, you may want to be cautious about what you are asked to do in the name of the friendship. You must realize that as the follower, you are subject to manipulation. Finally, you need to realize that a relationship will have its awkward moments until both parties recognize their roles.

There is another dimension of friendship role playing that merits your attention if you are to approach the subject with any kind of wisdom.

Some people bring out the best in their friends. Some bring out the worst. I have a friend who is a complainer. I don't know whether he does that as a way of life. I don't even know whether he complains around other people. But he complains when he is around me. And when we are together, we complain, we gripe, we bemoan our state, we feel sorry for ourselves, we spread negativism so thick that it takes me days to cut through enough to see the sunlight. Of course, since I am writing this, I am making him sound like the culprit—as if I am only being manipulated by him. But I know that is not true; I am as much to blame as he.

My complaining friend is not a bad man. He is loyal, kind, knowledgeable, conversant. I like him. But I don't like myself when I am with him. He brings out of me a dimension that I would just as soon leave buried. Some psychologists may protest that I shouldn't squelch my innermost thoughts, but I wouldn't have those thoughts if that complainer weren't there. When I know I am going to be with this person, I prepare myself. I think, *I'm not going to say anything.* But I always break that promise. So now, I am staying away from him as much as I can.

On the other hand, I have another friend I am not sure I even like. On the surface, it would seem that we have little in common. But when I am with him, I am wittier, happier, more satisfied, more profound, more imaginative. I don't know if I like him, but I like myself when I am with him.

Now, it is your time to be honest. Ask yourself these questions: *Which friends bring out the best in me? Which friends bring out the worst in me? What role do I play? What do I bring out in my friends?*

Degrees of Friendship

Like the temperature, friendships come in degrees running from cold to hot. On the college campus, there are four major friendship zones: (1) the "Have a nice day" zone; (2) the "Let's get together and study for the test" zone; (3) the "I know what let's do, let's steal all the toilet paper on campus and stash it in the dean's office" zone; (4) the "I don't like my life very much" zone.

1. The "Have a nice day" zone. During your college career, you will see thousands of faces. How many of those you remember well enough to attach a name to depends on what is important to you. Some people say, "Oh, I'm not good at names and faces," but that is probably not an accurate statement. They just don't rank this as important. Anybody who can remember the Latin names for all the bones in the body can remember names and faces.

Although these friendships lack the real depth from which great love stories are written, there are some advantages to accumulating some of them. For one thing, it may be rather impressive to someone that you are on first-name basis with Paul Popularity or Captain Football. At least, it won't hurt your ego, and it may help your image. These friendships also have the possibility of becoming permanent and through the years may grow some. In fact, I know several people who turned a "Have a nice day" zone into something much warmer after they graduated and left the place. The fact that you went to the same school, spent four years of your life in the same buildings with the same people, and lived through the same traditions gives you more in common than you will have with most people you will meet throughout your life.

Friendships on this degree are also safe. You can know a large number of people without really ever having to trust any of them with anything personal. There isn't much risk involved.

Of course, the dangers of operating entirely in this zone are obvious. Everybody has a need to get deeper than this with someone. Everybody has a need to trust someone and to be trusted by someone. In fact, these friendships can be rather deceptive. Frequently, the people who are best at accumulating the "Have a nice day" friends can be the loneliest people on campus. They are so socially active that no one takes time to trust them. Often, I have seen girls who were so popular that they never got asked out on dates. What a terrible feeling! To be lonely amidst all your friends.

I do hope if you operate in this zone, you are at least clever enough to come up with something other to say than that worn out, "Have a nice day." Just because you want to be casual is no reason for you to settle for inane.

I have some suggestions, just in passing of course.

"I hope you eat soon."

"I wish you clean socks every day."

"May your underwear always fit."

"I think I am in love with you."

"Hello. I am incredibly rich," or the totally new, "Think it'll rain?"

2. The "Let's get together and study for the test" zone. This particular zone is much warmer than the first and could even be more satisfying than zones 3 and 4. If you invite someone to study with you, you are obviously prepared to reveal one of two precious and very private aspects of your personality—your ignorance or your knowledge. It takes a good deal of trust for you to subject either to public scrutiny.

At the surface level, these are profitable friendships regardless of your role in the relationship. If you are the dumb one, you will obviously profit from your friend's expertise. If you are the bright one, you will profit from the responsibility of having to organize your information and insights into a teachable scheme.

There is one possible danger. There has to be some sharing in this kind of friendship. If you have a servant-type personality, you may find yourself doing all the intellectual work while your friend plays Joe College. If you find yourself sliding into this kind of arrangement, ask some serious questions about what you are gaining. It may be better for you to find another study buddy.

On the positive side, these friendships often develop into very rewarding, permanent relationships. It is quite possible that your lifelong friends will come from this zone, and from this, the friendship could go to zone 4.

For one thing, these friendships are based on solid ground. You have a tangible, obvious reason for getting together—the material you need to study. It is not as if you set a date then try to guess what each other wants to do to kill the two hours you allotted.

This study material is probably the most wholesome thing that will bring you together with your colleagues. You will probably spend most of your time talking about the material and sharing ideas rather than talking about people and sharing complaints. As long as you stay together and study, you won't get in trouble with the dean's office either.

3. The "I know what let's do . . ." zone. (Although I am listing these zones as separate categories, they do overlap with each other; and frequently, they will include the same people. I do think the categorization is valuable because it helps you identify your friendship needs.)

You need friends to help you through those serious, thoughtful moments such as when you first realize the creative genius behind the construction of the human eyeball. Those are meaningful moments that need to be shared with someone who will either appreciate or fake appreciation as much as you. But then, when that is over, you need friends to help you through the giddy moments when you play out your fantasies of being the world's greatest criminal mind or at least the world's greatest taker of risks. (It is important for me to mention these contrasting times in the same paragraph because I want you to realize that college life should be filled with both kinds of experiences. One of those times may receive more glamorous treatment than the other, but they are both satisfying when held in perspective and retrospective.)

With friends from this zone, you reveal another part of yourself—the flippant, childish side, the "I don't want to grow up just yet" side. And it is good to let that side get some exposure at times.

There are, as always, a couple of dangers. If you do not exercise good judgment, friends from this zone can steal too much of your time. Their appeal is inviting because it is actually rather comfortable. You don't have to be too trusting of any one person to participate in a mob pillow fight. Your personhood, the part of you that is symbolized by your fingerprints, can stay safely hidden during the fun times. But that isn't so when you are deeply engrossed in an intellectual conversation. You may be less vulnerable, less exposed, less naked when you are streaking through a campus pep rally than when you are talking about religion with a friend. The other danger in spending too much of your time with friends in this zone is that they may not always be loyal. If you are going to establish a permanent relationship with someone, the mutual cause will have to be something more significant than dropping water balloons out the third-floor window.

4. The "I don't like my life very much" zone. I supervise college seniors during their student teaching internships. For most of them, this is a difficult period emotionally, physically, and intellectually. They have to adjust to several new relationships. They have to stay up late preparing lessons. They have to establish quick rapport with high school students who don't respect student teachers very much. And there is always someone looking over their shoulder.

I prepare these students for the experience by telling them to form a close, rewarding relationship with a sensitive, caring, warm, understanding *post*. Yes, I said post. They need to talk to someone or something that will listen. They may need advice, but before they can accept advice, they need to talk.

One of the most crucial factors to your survival in college could be your finding that one person who will listen to you when you need to bare your soul. Don't deceive yourself. Those times will come—the times when you leave tear stains on the pillowcase. For most people, the best therapy for those times is being able to unload those problems on someone else.

If this were a scientific book, I would now get into a discussion of the credentials for that person or persons whom you choose to listen to your life's story. But I think the most important credential is obvious. The person must be able to listen, and you must trust him.

Regardless of what you call this person—counselor, listener, confessor, or friend—he plays a vital role in your college experience.

Again, there are dangers. One danger is that you may get to where you enjoy telling someone about your misery. This happens. We find a listening soul, and by pouring out our burdens, we find we are actually manipulating him. Since manipulation is a form of power and power is a pill for the depression we were feeling in the first place, we become rather adept at staying miserable enough to keep the story interesting. Too much of this will destroy your college experience and you with it.

On the other hand, you may find yourself on the listening end of such a relationship. Be careful of what I am saying here. I am not suggesting that you be cruel, insensitive, or rude; but there is a fine line between being sympathetic and being manipulated. Just make sure that you don't let another person's burdens jeopardize your own survival.

Friendships in this zone can be very time-consuming, so you must be careful about how many of these you establish.

Variety

Before I conclude this chapter on this very important aspect to surviving and thriving in college, let me remind you of another delightful possibility of college friendships—variety. The typical college campus offers you about as many flavors as most ice cream stores do. Now is the time for you to get acquainted with some people who at first glance look a little different. Don't deny yourself a great opportunity. Cultivate some friendships with people who are racially, nationally, or physically different from you and your other friends. You may find these quite rewarding.

When I was in college, I established a friendship with a blind student. Not only are memories of my college days richer because of that friendship, but my education is more complete.

This is the purpose of college friends. They will make the experience fun as you are going through it, and they will contribute to the quality of the rest of your life.

4

Dating

Under the best conditions, dating is tricky business. Writing about dating is even trickier. To write some explanation of this complex and personal activity, I have to deal in generalities; and as soon as I do, you will say, "I'm not like that at all. Who does he think he is to make such statements?"

Well, I hope you *are* different, because that means that you understand yourself and your own dating needs. If you understand those things, you are on your way to having successful dating experiences in college because you know how to define *successful.* But if you are not so sure, let me offer some observations—general observations.

The Differences at College

You probably already have some ideas about your dating life which you have gathered from past experience or from reading about the subject. Generally, that information is applicable to the college campus. But there are a couple of aspects to college dating that set it apart from any previous dating you may have done.

First, college dating often tends to be "terminal." In other words, college daters often end up marrying each other. That's not bad. I'm not condemning it. I'm just reporting. In fact, that practice makes a lot of sense to me. Educated people who have shared similar educational experiences should have a lot in common. They should be able to build solid marriages.

But this piece of information is also a warning. Since the college campus is occasionally a mating ground, you need to consider your choice of dates rather seriously. This could be the person you marry. Now, I know I left out some important steps in between, but some first dates do lead to marriages. Yours might.

I doubt that any guy ever called a girl and said, "Let's go out Friday night; and if everything works out, we'll get married." I doubt that anybody ever said this, but it is a possibility in every dating proposal offered. Both parties need to know this.

College dating also offers the opportunity for a relationship to become intense. It is a simple matter of time. The campus situation allows two people to spend just about as much time with each other as they want; and because of this time together, the relationship may grow intense before either person really intended it to.

The problem with this is that it is deceptive. Frequently it happens this way: Two freshmen meet and go out on the first date—a simple little outing to a campus activity, perhaps. Since they feel comfortable with each other, they begin to meet for meals; they wait for each other after class; they go to the library and study together. Soon, they are inseparable, and at this point, the relationship is intense, whether either person wanted it to get that way or not.

"What's wrong with that?" you ask. Well, a relationship that grows too quickly will either burn itself out or it will force the daters to alter their plans to accommodate the relationship.

Before you get into such a situation, you need to remember a couple of points. All living things grow. In fact, that is one of the characteristics of living things. (I pass that piece of information on to you should you ever need it for a biology exam.) If a relationship is alive, it is growing. When it stops growing, it dies.

A dating relationship grows in a series of emotional and physical steps. (Yes, I said *physical.*) They spot each other across the room in psychology class. For days, they play the staring game, staring while the other isn't looking, trying not to get caught, but hoping they do. Finally, he asks her out. We have just achieved step one. They hold hands, and we have achieved step two. They kiss, and we have gone through step three. Soon, this couple is faced with a major decision. They are going to have to decide how far they are going with those physical steps, or they will have to stop seeing each other.

Obviously, this warning comes from the old-fashioned morality which says that sex outside of marriage is bad. I confess. I believe that strongly. You may say, "Of course, he does. After all, he is a religious person." Well, that is true. I do have religious feelings about the subject—strong feelings. Both the Bible and the universal laws of human decency are very clear here. Human sexuality is a precious part of creation, but it is one that is to be guarded and even restricted. Ours is a monogamous society. Fidelity in love is an uncompromising virtue. Sex outside of marriage is immoral, and it carries with it all the social, emotional, and spiritual repercussions of immorality.

But I could also base the above warning on a very practical principle. For the past twenty years, I have observed that young people who don't engage in sex have fewer problems than those who do. I have scores of illustrations to support that observation—illustrations of young people just like you who spent too much of their adolescence being unhappy because of their sexual activity. The pleasures of sex are so temporary, so fleeting, that they just don't justify the risks.

Because of this, I strongly urge college daters to regulate the speed at which the relationship grows. If you still have three years of college left and you can't afford both school and a spouse, avoid an intense relationship. Monitor the time you spend together. Spread the growth steps over a three-year period.

On smaller campuses, the community itself contributes to the intensity of the relationship. If a couple dates two or three times, the rumors spread, and outsiders honor the relationship. In other words, in the eyes of the campus, the relationship is serious whether the couple knows it or not.

Long Live the Differences

Now that I've frightened you with these precautions, let me be positive. College dating is not only fun, it can also be a valuable educational experience, particularly if you look at dating as an opportunity to learn something about the opposite sex.

That statement will probably provoke a lot of rebuttal from those people who don't believe there is that much difference between men and women. But let's be realistic. Whether sex roles are learned or innate, they still exist; and if you are going to survive in a world where both sexes interact at several levels, you need to learn to feel comfortable around members of the opposite sex. That is one of the objects of dating. That is how you can justify the time you spend on the activity.

Before I list some specific suggestions to facilitate the learning process, let me make one general observation. There is a rather popular myth in our society that dating is the process of searching for someone who needs the very same thing from a relationship that you need. Once you find that person, the two of you can live the rest of your lives in complete harmony, satisfying each other's common needs.

Well, I hope it works that way for you. I also hope you inherit a new Porsche and find gold at the end of the rainbow. But I don't have any of those things and I am still happy. My wife and I have been married for twenty-four years—nearly a quarter of a century. She has certain needs in our marriage, and I have a completely different set of needs. They are not the same at all. In fact, sometimes our needs oppose each other.

Last night I invited students to our house for dinner. My wife did not need to have those students to cook and clean for. Instead, she needed sleep. But she stayed up until midnight, washing dinner dishes. Why did she do that? Because I needed to have the students in our home, and she loves me enough to make some personal sacrifices to help me meet my needs. She hopes I will do the same for her. And that is what love is—responding to the other person's needs because you know your needs will be met when the time comes. You need to understand that while you are still young and you are still in the dating stage. Two people in any relationship will not have the same needs. If the relationship is to work, there will have to be some give-and-take.

It may help you to understand what the other person is expecting from the relationship, so let me make some general suggestions from both sides. Your heartthrob may not fit into my generalities; but at least you will have some background.

From His Side of the Fence

1. Guys like girls who are girls. Most guys like feminine, frilly things. (I know it is crazy for me to say this, but I must be realistic.) In other words, guys like pretty girls! If you are having trouble getting asked out, you might begin by throwing away the painter pants and combat boots and brushing your hair one hundred times every night. Let's face it. Pretty is not only physiological, it can be an attitude. If you decide to make yourself attractive, you will probably become attractive.

2. Some guys don't date because they can't afford it. Unfortunately, some college students get the idea that anything that costs less than forty dollars isn't a date. I don't know who started this—the guys or the girls. But the guys have to pay for it; so the girls don't get asked out as much. If you can think of a date as a walk around the park or a trip to the library, you might throw some hints. Somebody may be rather interested in you, but he just doesn't have the forty dollars.

3. Some guys don't like group dates. Don't be disappointed if not all guys are really enthusiastic about these types of dates.

4. Guys like to feel masculine. (I will really get in trouble for this, but I still think it is true.) There is something called the male ego. (There is also something called the female ego.) If the guy is not getting his ego fed when he is with you, he may as well be out with the boys. When he takes you to the football game, act interested. If he says, "They're going to pass," you say, "Oh, what's a pass?"

Don't say, "Pass? On third and three with the defense in a seven-deep umbrella zone—you must be crazy!" Play it cool. Let him think he is the expert on that subject.

From Her Side of the Fence

1. Girls don't like wrestling matches. Some might, but most don't. If you get a reputation as a grappler, you may meet a lot of girls who have to stay in and study.

2. Girls tend to enjoy large group dates. Participate in some. You may find the activity rather refreshing.

3. Girls aren't as impulsive as guys. They need more time to anticipate and prepare for a big event like a date, so ask several days beforehand.

4. But on the other hand, don't be afraid to be spontaneous.

5. Don't be afraid to be creative. Just because everyone else is spending large bankrolls on every date is no reason for you to. Think of something totally different that won't cost you anything; then ask a girl. If she doesn't want to go, she will tell you.

Obviously, a general list like this won't include all the information you will need if you are going to understand something as unique as another human being—particularly when that human being is of the opposite sex.

My only objective here—in this whole chapter in fact—is to give you some encouragement and confidence. College dating is a little different from other dating you might have done, but it is close enough for you to apply the same principles.

Dating is an integral part of college life, and I encourage you to participate, even if it is the group kind. There is an educational value in learning how to develop relationships with the opposite sex. Some people find dating recreational, a pleasant pastime. And some even meet their mates in college. In fact, that's what happened to me.

5

Parents

Before we conclude this discussion on the people who can help you survive and thrive in college, let me mention a couple of others—your parents. In the midst of your roommate activities, your various friendships, and your frequent or rare dates, don't forget your parents.

By now, you are probably saying, "What kind of reminder is this—don't forget my parents? I won't do that. This man must be some kind of a nut to advise me not to forget my parents."

Well, I hope you are more accurate than I, but my student advisors on this project asked me to include a chapter on the subject. Most of them reported that in the process of getting involved in the studies and social life of college, they had not maintained as close a relationship with their parents as they now wished they had. I am simply offering you this advice before you accumulate some regrets of your own.

What Are Patterns For?

As I listened to my advisors talk about their relationships with their parents, I began to detect a rather common pattern. I will discuss the pattern here; then you can use it to analyze where you are in your own relationship with your parents.

1. Homesickness. For many freshmen, the first reaction having to do with their parents is homesickness. I realize that is rather childish sounding for such a sophisticated audience. Homesickness is what children get when they go to scout camp. So let's use another term—*severance pains.* Actually, severance pain may be a more accurate term than homesickness.

If you are normal, there will come a time during those first few weeks when you realize that you don't live at home anymore. There will be subtle hints. Your mother turns your room into a sewing room. Your father drops you from the family car insurance policy. Someone throws away your old toothbrush. Your heartthrob back home starts dating someone else.

When you get enough of these subtle hints, you suddenly realize that life goes forward. It doesn't stand still, and it doesn't go backward. Your past was comfortable because you knew what was going on, but the future is a mysterious unknown.

When you couple this insight into the nature of life with the normal problems of adjusting to college, you will suffer severance pains (homesickness to a scout).

2. Withdrawal. The most common therapy for homesickness is to forget about home—to throw yourself full force into college activities and just quit remembering the past. When you do that, you will stop communicating with your parents on a regular basis. Soon, there will be so much about your new life that you haven't told them that you will find it easier not to share anything substantial. By now, the relationship is casual, perhaps even ceremonial. You love your parents, but you just don't seem to have much in common anymore.

3. Rebuilding. But if you are still normal, there will come a time (according to my advisors) when you will need to rebuild what has disappeared from lack of use. There will come a time when you will need a closer relationship with your parents.

Near the end of your college career, you are going to make several major decisions that could have significant bearing on the quality of the rest of your life—decisions about profession, geographical location, and maybe even a mate. When you make those decisions, it is good to get as much advice as you can, but it is especially good to get your parents' blessing.

My father died when I was thirty-one years old. At that time, I realized that I had never made a major purchase (house, car, furniture) without first gaining his approval. That is why you need to keep a close relationship with those people you respect the most.

Why the Pattern?

Actually, this pattern in the relationship with your parents may be logical when you consider what happens to you during your college career.

When you go to college at eighteen, you will be an adolescent, a mere child. When you finish at twenty-two, you will be an adult. I don't know how that process occurs. You won't even know when it is happening to you, but when you come out of college, you will be much closer to your parents' age than you were when you went in.

Part of the process of that maturity includes defining your own beliefs. When you are young, you believe most of what you believe because someone *told* you to believe it—because of authority models in your life. When you mature, you begin to *choose* what you want to believe. In order to make intelligent choices, you first have to deny the authority figures who have been responsible for your belief patterns. That is when you sever strong relationships with your parents.

But once you have confirmed your own beliefs, you can respect the opinions of those authorities again. As that famous comedian, Almost Everyone, once said, "When I was eighteen, I was appalled at how dumb my father was, but when I was twenty-two, I was impressed with how much the old man had learned in four years."

Incidentally, this process of confirming your own beliefs is frequently very painful. I will discuss it more fully in chapter 7, but I want to mention it here because of its impact on your relationship with your parents.

Keeping a Firm Hold

Obviously the above explanation for the pattern of student–parent relationships is not comprehensive. There are many possible reasons for the distance that comes between the two and for the attempts to bridge the distance later. But I would like for you to begin to think about some of the changes you will probably encounter during the time you are trying to survive and thrive in college and about what those changes could mean to your past relationships, including those with your parents. I also want to remind you, convincingly if I can, of my original thesis for this chapter, "For best results during your college career, keep a close fellowship with your parents."

I have some suggestions to help you meet that goal.

1. Keep your parents posted. That last word is short for *post office.* Use it. Actually, it's a fairly good invention from the Ben Franklin era, and it has served the American people well (despite the bad publicity). Grit your teeth and get into the habit. You may find it painless and even pleasant after a while.

I'll be specific. Fit letter writing into your schedule. Promise yourself a minimum (e.g., I'll write my parents once a week). Then stick to your promise. If the weekly letter is not written by show time Saturday night, deny yourself the movie until you have a few lines scribbled. You will be amazed at how fast you can get the weekly message out.

Of course, at times you may want to impress your parents with quality, but consistency is a virtue as well. When you are in a writing mood, author that masterpiece which will be shown around to all the friends and relatives and then preserved in the family Bible. But when you are not in a writing mood, any old note is better than nothing. As a parent, I assure you that joy comes from just getting an envelope from the child away at school.

If you are really into consistency, you may want to discover postcards. They are relatively inexpensive and they are quick. You can carry some of those things around in your pocket and fill one up while the physics teacher is calling role. Presto! You can share a daily highlight with your parents. I would particularly encourage you to use postcards if your parents are lonely for some reason. If you are the last child to leave home or if you come from a one-parent family or if your parents are hurting for some reason, your small note could be the highlight of the day. Think about that. College is not a place to develop personal selfishness. And a daily postcard could not only help you keep a diary, it could also help someone share the experience with you.

You may also want to consider other forms of printed communication with your parents. If you are in the habit of getting your name in the campus newspaper, put your parents on the subscription list. Or at least, send them the issue that announces you won the intramural tiddlywink championship.

Of course, there are other ways to keep your parents posted, but since I am trying to hold down my telephone bills, I won't mention those.

2. Share your highs as well as your lows—your lows as well as your highs. Frequently, we gravitate to one relationship or another depending on how we feel. When we are up, we seek out old Chuckling Charlie for a rousing good time. When we are down, we look for Sympathetic Sam. Occasionally, there are people in our lives who support us during all moods. Parents probably fall into that category. At least, as parents they have a right to know about our moods and to volunteer their support.

When you go away to college and have a long-distance relationship with your parents (via the telephone or writing), it is easy to let the relationship slip into a one-dimensional one, and you find yourself only communicating when you are hurting; or on the other hand, you may try to bear your hurts alone and only let your parents in on the happy times. That is why consistency in writing and calling is so important. You really need to let your parents see the balance. You need to let them know that you are somewhere within the boundaries of normal—that you get happy and you get sad, that you experience achievements as well as setbacks.

If you have kept this balanced relationship with your parents, you will find that they can offer more intelligent support when the time comes for you to be supported. They will be able to offer wiser counsel about the weighty decisions that come near the end of the college career. They will be able to offer greater understanding when your life and grades crumble at the same time and your pillowcase gets damp.

Just for exercise in establishing and perpetuating a balanced relationship, why don't you sit down and write them a note telling them that you *don't* need money. That information ought to provide some real surprises.

3. Visit your parents during vacation. Now, reread that heading and put some emphasis on the first word. I am serious. *Visit* your parents, and visit *with* your parents.

Sure. I know how you are looking forward to the semester break when you can journey back to the old hometown for two fun-filled weeks of freedom from study and of sleeping in your old bed and of eating Mom's cooking and of renewing the old friendships.

I know all about your good intentions, but I also know what

happens far too frequently. I know about those cool college kids who dash in the front door, hug Mom and Dad, throw six months of dirty clothes at Mom's feet for her expert attention, borrow the keys to the car, and disappear into the bowels of the hometown until it is time to gather up the clean clothes and go back to the books.

In the midst of your frantic activity to reestablish all those high school friendships and in the midst of those temptations to play Joe or Jane College in the hangouts all over town, plan some time for your parents. Plan to spend some time just with them when you can sit down and say all those things you can't say in letters—the moods, the feelings, the frustrations, the setbacks. Your parents may be more interested in those things than you think; and if they are interested they have a right to know them— to help you feel and experience. That is part of the joy of parenthood. So help them to remain a part of you. Visit.

4. Help your parents understand what is happening to you. As I said earlier, you will probably undergo some changes during your college career. You will enter as an adolescent and emerge as an adult. Not only do you need to understand that, but your parents need to know also. Discuss this with them. Prepare them for the inevitable changes in your relationship that will come as you mature. You may begin by asking them to read this chapter.

To conclude this chapter, let me repeat the thesis. During your college career, you will meet, befriend, date, like, dislike, study with, and play with a variety of people. These relationships are a valuable part of your education, perhaps almost as important as classes themselves.

But in the excitement of meeting so many new people, don't forget those people who have loved you the longest. Don't forget your parents. When it's all over, when all the tears have been shed and all the professors have been hugged and all the decisions have been made, you may find that your parents have been your best friends all the time.

6

Extracurricular Activities

Notice how that term *extracurricular activities* conjures up images of three-hundred-pound football players, eight-foot basketball giants, the world's sweetest horn blowers, and future Oscar winners singing the lead in *Oklahoma*.

If that is the vision you get from the term, you have probably already built up your defenses against this chapter, and you are daring me to convince you that you have the necessary size and talent to participate in college extracurricular activities.

I am going to accept that dare. I am going to propose that if you are going to survive and thrive in college you do need to find a place to participate. I am going to suggest that participation in an extracurricular activity is almost necessary to your maintaining a healthy outlook toward yourself and your obligations during your college career. Find an activity and get involved.

In order to implement that suggestion, you need to consider two points. First, you may need to broaden your definition of extracurricular activity, and then you must be cautious about underestimating your size and talent before you have had a chance to take a good look at what college activities demand.

Broadening the Definition

I define an extracurricular activity as anything outside your classwork that can use your time and talent. Consider the implications for a moment. On your campus, regardless of where you choose to go to college, there is some organization that needs what you can do. It may be as obvious as the football team or the women's chorale. Or maybe the local convalescent home needs volunteers to visit. Nevertheless, something on campus needs you. Understanding this helps with choice. The appropriate extracurricular activity is the one that has the greatest need of what you can do for it.

How do you find the activity that is just waiting until you come along? Read, ask, and experiment. First, begin by reading the campus literature, including the posters. You will notice announcements (and sometimes pleas) of club meetings and activities. If you are looking for a particular type of organization, don't be afraid to ask. Go to the student affairs office or the student union office or some agency assigned the task of keeping track of all clubs and activities on campus. See what looks good.

After you have found something that appeals to you, attend a meeting. Get involved. If you find that you don't fit in, try something else. But find yourself an extracurricular activity.

Values of Participation

I could remind you of the obvious values of extracurricular activities—you can meet people, you can get a break from your studies, you can learn something about groups and activities—but my recommendation is based on another value. Extracurricular participation can give you an opportunity to feel worthwhile.

College is something of a self-serving activity. You are using up space, air, and water while you concentrate on your own problems, classes, and studies. You know that when you finish, you are going to make the world a better place to be, but you would like some practice during those four years while you are in the holding pattern.

This conflict between preparing yourself to be useful in the future and being useful in the present causes some serious tension among many college students. In fact, I know several who have experienced the tension so critically that they have dropped out and altered their plans while seeking some way of being of service to mankind.

All of us need to feel that we are of some worth. Finding the right extracurricular activity could provide you with just enough incentive that you can even tackle your studies with greater enthusiasm because you see the purpose for what you are doing.

This is valuable for both your mental and physical health. Several years ago I was affiliated with a high school that emphasized a wide range of active, successful extracurricular programs which utilized nearly every student in school. We set all sorts of good attendance records. When students had some reason, some need to come to school beyond just going to class, they weren't sick as often. Such an activity might be the very thing to help you through your college days.

Yes, You Can!

I also suggest that you not underestimate your talent too quickly. Some college activity may need you more than you suspect. A few years ago, I helped coach a college football team that featured an all-conference defensive safety. This young man was bright, consistent, and inspirational. He held down the safety spot on our team from his sophomore through his senior years.

So what kind of high school hero was he to play such an important role on the college team? all-state? all-conference?—he didn't even start. He ran down on kickoffs and played when the coach was trying to hold down the score.

How do we account for his success as a college player? He *matured* into the position. If he can do it, so can you.

Don't underestimate yourself. If you think you want to try something, try it. If you aren't good enough, someone will tell you; but you will never know until you try. Don't spend the rest of your life wondering whether you were good enough to play on the baseball team or to sing in the musical. Find out. If you make it, celebrate. If you don't, you have still learned what it is like to participate.

But It's Not All Roses!

As with everything, extracurricular participation comes with some warnings on the label. These activities should provide you with release from tension and stress; they should not create more. If you find that your extracurricular activity is demanding too much of your actual or emotional time, you may want to rethink your priorities.

Be careful of that warning because it contradicts the popular present-day myth which says scholarships to participate in extracurricular activities are the greatest blessing that could come to a college student. I understand how participation scholarships in sports, music, drama, or whatever work; and I am happy for the people who win them. But be assured that this is not a trouble-free way to get through college. If you are good enough to win a scholarship, congratulations. But if you accept a scholarship, you must also accept the burdens of time, emotional strain, and energy drain that participation carries. I warn you. Don't let the extracurricular activity add unbearable burdens to your schedule and don't forget why you came to college in the first place.

Extracurricular participation can offer you friends, fellowship, educational experiences, and a positive attitude about yourself, but the participation should help you survive and thrive—not hinder you.

7

Moral Principles

Last night I sat for three hours and laughed until my sides hurt. I was listening to a couple of graduates of one of the most conservative and prestigious Bible schools in the nation swap stories about the practical jokes they had masterminded during their college days.

One thing was certain. No one had cheated them out of a good time just because they had been students at a Bible school. They had fun, and they had recorded enough happy and uproarious memories to last a lifetime. And they had done all this without alcohol, drugs, sex, abusing anyone, or cheating on their scholarship.

I use this story to introduce this chapter on moral integrity because I want you to know that I think people ought to have a good time. In fact, that is one of the reasons why you ought to go to college. While you are there, you should work at accumulating enough memories to last through forty years of retelling.

But I don't think you have to take chances with your future or go against your own moral code. I think you can enjoy yourself and catalog a whole list of happy times; and still come out with your moral character intact.

That is the thesis of this chapter. Thus far, we have discussed the social interactions of college life—roommates, friends, members of the opposite sex, partners in extracurricular activities, and parents. We have talked about the values and some of the possible dangers of these social relationships. As a conclusion to this section on social interaction, I want to remind you that these relationships on the college campus will not only provide you with good times, but they will also probably present a constant test of your own moral code—of what you really stand for as a human being—of what you will tolerate and what you won't—of what you will sacrifice and what you won't.

Like any other exam, you need to prepare for this test before you get to it. The college experience will offer such a unique combination of liberty and variety of moral decisions that you need to think about those decisions before you get to them. For the first time in your life (probably) you will be totally responsible for your own actions, and you will face this freedom of choice in the midst of a wide assortment of beckoning influences ranging from the goody-goody to the totally depraved. You need to think about this and make some decisions before you get locked into the emergency of the situation and find yourself living a life-style you don't really endorse.

The Moral Boundary

The first place for you to begin preparing for this exam is to come to some understanding about what moral actions are. Where is the boundary between morality and immorality, and when, if ever, can you step across that boundary?

At this point, I may as well tell you that I think there is a difference between morality and immorality—that there are accepted patterns of behavior and individual actions that are moral and others that are immoral. I believe that the boundary between the two has been established through the principles of God and through the laws of human decency.

In other words, there is an intelligent way to live, and there is a foolish way to live.

Before you go to college and are presented with the various options of the college experience, you need to have some sense of where that boundary is and some personal conviction about how far—if at all—you can step over it. This sense and conviction comprise your moral code.

It is not my intention to be completely dogmatic at this point because a moral code isn't of any value unless it is yours, unless you have developed it yourself and made an agreement with yourself that you will live by its tenets. That is why it is important for you to establish your own moral code before you are confronted with the various options of the college experience.

Perhaps I can help you establish some general principles without breaking my vow not to be dogmatic. It seems to me that immorality can be divided into three categories: (1) It is immoral to abuse your body, your mind, or your own emotions. (2) It is immoral to take advantage of another person. (3) It is immoral to break a contract.

Some Challenges to the Boundary

Recently several middle-aged people have enjoyed telling me the same joke. A man at his retirement dinner announced, "If I had known I was going to live this long, I would have taken better care of myself." The joke is funnier to us in middle age than it is to you because we are beginning to pay the price of reckless youth. We are becoming conscious of the fact that this body is a single-issue affair. If we wear this one out, we don't get another. If we let our own body rust, we can't strip and repaint the way we do with cars. This is it. We have to live with what we have.

If I ruin my eyes by misuse or improper care, I will just have to go through life not seeing as well as I would like. If I ruin my ears with too much loud noise, I will just have to go through life not hearing as well as I should. If I put drugs or alcohol into my body in such proportions that I mess up the system, I will just have to live with a damaged system.

This same thing applies to your mind, your emotions, and your reputation. If you mess them up, you have affected the quality of the rest of your life.

Fortunately, most college students are wise enough to make the adjustment to the liberty and variety of the moral choices without causing any damage. Sometimes they have to alter some of their actions during the experience, but most make it. Recently, a senior told me that as a freshman, he was so overwhelmed with all the freedom that he began to drink. Soon, he was drinking heavily every night. His grades suffered for lack of study time, and his mind lost its sharpness. Finally, he realized that this was not the best use of his one shot to perfect his abilities; so he transferred to another school and quit drinking entirely.

You can't abuse your body, mind, or emotions just because the college campus offers you the opportunity to do so. You must have a moral line—a boundary that will protect you from destroying yourself.

Risk and Experimentation

Now, I am realistic enough to recognize that, despite all my good advice, you will probably do some experimenting. You want to find out some things for yourself. You want to establish your own moral boundaries and not rely on mine.

I recognize your need to experiment, to take some risks, and it is not my intention to deny you educational or fun experiences. But that is why I insist on the importance of your having established that moral line before you get to college. Know what you can allow yourself to do. Know how far you can go before you needlessly jeopardize the rest of your life. Know where you can get the courage to say no to the group and stand firmly on your own personal moral codes.

At this point, you are probably putting together a defense to this which sounds something like, "But won't I be a social outcast? Isn't it necessary for me to take liberties with my body, mind, and life in order to be socially accepted on campus?"

I answer with an emphatic and resounding NO! And that answer is based on something far more solid than middle-aged morality. I talk to lots of college students, and they assure me that popularity is in no way attached to lax moral standards. Regardless of where you go to school, you can find a crowd of friends who will respect your commitments and life-style.

College girls who don't submit to sexual advances and propositions have just as many dates as they would if they did, and they are definitely in a healthier emotional state.

There are just as many parties and social activities where people are sober as there are the other kind. If your friends encourage you to use drugs, including alcohol, or if they ridicule you for not doing so, you have the wrong friends. Quit that bunch and find some others. This is the point I am making in this whole section on social relationships: Somewhere there are people who will accept you for what you are, for the uniqueness represented by the tips of your fingers. Your job is to find them.

I remind you of the illustration about the Bible college graduates at the beginning of this chapter. I suspect that one reason college students engage in immoral activities is lack of imagination. Planning a drunken orgy doesn't demand any great brilliance. But putting a Volkswagen in the hall of the third floor of the administration building requires some strategy. And the next morning, you will have more than a headache and a guilty conscience. You will have a work of art and a memory suitable for telling your grandchildren.

I repeat my concern. College is more than a childish romp. During those four years, you will make the transition from adolescent to adult. Going into the experience, you are probably focusing your attention on the adolescent experimentation. But remember that when you come out of the experience, you will be an adult. In other words, during those four years, you are doing more than experimenting. You are actually establishing a lifestyle that will accompany you for years.

For example, during my own college years, I lost discipline in eating habits. I gained twenty pounds, and I have been between twenty and eighty pounds overweight ever since. As you establish your own moral code for college, as you decide what you will or will not participate in, ask yourself, *How will this look when I am forty?*

A Source of Moral Fiber: Final Note

Before I end this discussion of moral character and actions, I accept my moral obligation to tell you where you can get the inner strength to live by your own code. Once you have decided what your life is going to stand for, how do you meet your own expectations?

Thus far, I have tried to present a case for a practical strength. You can live by your own principles because it is sensible to do so. Your thoughts of the future will direct the present.

However, this may not always be sufficient to keep you from something you will later regret. I must confess the practical side alone wouldn't work for me. Instead, I gain what inner strength I have through a commitment to my Creator. If I can stop every day and reflect on what God did at the time of Creation and what Christ did at His Crucifixion and Resurrection—if I can stop every day and reflect on the uniqueness that God breathed into me when He put me together—if I can reflect on these things, I can get enough courage, discipline, and strength to live through that day. Then I just have to do it all again tomorrow.

This is what I call the devotional life. I recommend that you give it a try on a regular basis. You may find it valuable equipment as you survive and even thrive on college experiences.

Friends and Studies: The Bridge Between

Obviously, I think the social aspect of college is important. That is why I have put these six chapters on managing those relationships first in the book. I expect you to meet and have fun with some stimulating people. But I also think it is important for you to pass your classes and learn something in the process. That is why I dedicated the second section to those activities. But in both the social and the learning processes, your devotional life could be the permeating agent that brings quality and satisfaction to every experience.

If you need some practical, applicable advice for managing a difficult social relationship, search the Bible. Its principles are clear and workable. If you need some strength to establish your moral code, contemplate the nature of God. If you need the wisdom to know how to study and live harmoniously at the same time, try the power in prayer. If you take time to honor your devotional needs, you may discover the difference between surviving and thriving.

Part II

THE ACADEMIC ACTIVITIES

8

Professors

Besides your roommate and maybe a friend or two, professors are the most conspicuous animals you will meet at college. If you are going to survive and thrive in the classroom, you need to learn how to stalk these beasts.

Actually, the procedure isn't tough if you can remember one simple principle. In fact, your whole college education can be so much easier and more pleasant if you can master one simple concept—*professors are human*.

I realize there is some resistance to that idea, perhaps even from some professors' own family members, but the point stands. Professors are real people. They eat, sleep, laugh, and itch. They have likes and dislikes, and they make mistakes. Just because someone earns the right to sign his name with a bunch of funny letters behind it, doesn't mean he has lost his right to be human.

You probably think I am being absurd here, but I am quite serious. I am emphasizing this because I want to make a point. Your whole college experience will be so much freer of stress and anxiety if you can just realize that professors, regardless of all their degrees and honors and publications, are human.

I personally had trouble with this point throughout most of my higher education. Until I received one myself, I always had too much respect for people with Ph.D's. I always let that "Dr." in front of their names get in the way of my having a simple, person-to-person relationship with any of my professors. When I finally earned a degree myself, I suddenly realized that it wasn't any big deal. I am still the same human goof-up I was before the letters came.

The Personalizing Process

So the first task in mastering your college classwork is to find some way to personalize your professors—to get them out from behind their lecterns and spectacles so that you can realize that they have fingerprints and uniqueness too. To help you in this process, I have some suggestions. Remember as you read this list, that I am a professor myself; so you are getting this straight from the mouth of one of the animals. I know what works with me, and since I am human, I suspect it will work with my colleagues.

1. Choose your professors carefully. For several of your courses, you will probably have some choice of professors. In this case, you need to make a wise decision. You need to match yourself as student to the professor who comes closest to meeting your needs. To do this, you need two pieces of information: What kind of student are you? and What kind of teacher is that person?

You can get the answer to the second question by asking any of several people. You can always ask older students. News travels fast across college campuses, so almost everybody is fairly well posted about almost everybody else, particularly on important matters such as who is an easy professor for a required course.

Or you can ask an advisor. The advisor's information will be a bit less straightforward than that you get from older students; but if you read between the big words, you usually get about the same information. After all, the advisors get their information by listening to the older students.

But before you ask anyone the second question, you need to

know the answer to the first, "What kind of student are you?"

"Who is a good professor?" is not a good question so avoid asking it. For one thing, it is too blunt. More accurately, a good professor for one student may not be a good professor for another. Know enough about yourself to be able to ask intelligent questions. I can provide some examples.

A. Which professor gives the most extensive reading assignments? A professor is going to get content for his course from one of two sources—the reading assignments or his own mind. If he assigns many readings, then reading is more important than the class sessions. On the other hand, if a professor has fewer reading assignments, he will make up the difference through the quantity of material presented in class. Now, your problem is to decide whether you are a reader or a listener. How do you prefer to get your information? If you read accurately and fast, you may prefer the reading professor. If you are a slow reader, you may prefer the lecturer.

B. Does he put more emphasis on objective exams or papers? Usually this piece of information will reveal more about the professor than just the way he evaluates. Most professors who use objective exams exclusively are more interested in facts than arguments. They want you to get the information whether you like it or not. On the other hand, professors who use essay exams or papers are usually more open to your ideas and interpretations. If you have a mind that stores information easily and accurately, you will prefer the objective person. But if you think you are persuasive and equipped with the gift of gab, you will prefer the teacher who puts more emphasis on papers.

There is a word of caution here. Some professors are becoming quite skillful at writing complex, tricky, and thought-provoking objective exams. Some true–false tests can be real headaches, and those multiple-choice affairs which offer eight choices including "all of the above" and "none of the above" can bring saltwater stains to the pillowcase.

C. Is the professor organized or disorganized? All of us need some scheme for sorting through the material, but some professors use more illustrations than others. (Students sometimes call this "getting off the subject.") You can make this decision on your own.

D. Is his class straight lecture, or does he play some games? Game-playing classes can be fun and quite educational, but game playing always demands social interaction. Those classes demand that you learn the material while in a social setting. If you are the kind of person who works best alone, you should stay away from those as much as possible. On the other hand, if you are trolling for a date to the Christmas party, such a class will give you an opportunity to meet someone with whom you already have something in common.

You may want to add to this list, but these questions will at least get you started on the process of proper professor selection.

2. Discover your professor's academic interests. If your professor has a doctorate, he has written a dissertation (a book-length piece of work explaining his research findings). There is a little blurb about his dissertation in something called *Dissertation Abstracts.* If you are a serious student or if you are interested in shortcuts, you will find it profitable to go to the library during the early stages of the class and find that blurb. It is worth your time. You will not only understand what interests this person, but you may even work some reference into a class response. That should impress him and raise the anxiety level of all the other students in the class.

3. Meet your professor face to face. This is the most serious and important piece of advice in the entire book. In the early stages of the semester, get in to see every professor and try to develop a one-to-one relationship.

I know the value of this because I have it played on me all the

time. Every semester some serious student waltzes into my office
and says something like, "Hello. I am Gladys Goodgrade. I am
in your educational philosophy class. Yesterday I missed the
point when you referred to Rousseau's love life." She and I both
know that the reference was completely insignificant—just a
passing remark. But what is important is what she is really saying:
"Listen, Buster, I sit in third row, second seat. Smile the next
time you call my name." And I do. I will remember Gladys
Goodgrade the rest of the term—every time I need to ask a
question in class, every time I grade a paper or an exam, I will
remember that name.

Now you can manufacture your own need to get into your
professor's office where it is just the two of you—one on one:
your seat is too far from the chalkboard, your seat is too near the
chalkboard, you are left-handed in a right-handed chair (I got to
use that one all through college), you like his class, or you missed
a point.

By getting in to see the professor you have accomplished two
things. He will know you better and you will know him better.
Going into a professor's office is an education in itself. Usually, a
person's office decorations will reflect his personality.

4. If your professor invites the class to his home, go. Even if you
have to make a sacrifice, you should go. The more you see this
person in a human situation, the easier it will be for you to accept
his instruction and evaluation.

5. Invite your professor to your place. On our campus, many older
students (seniors) live in apartments. Frequently, my wife and I
are invited to some student's apartment for a meal. This is not
bribery. It is just a procedure for both professor and student to
learn that each is human. If you don't have an apartment, maybe
you could invite a professor to "open floor" in your dorm or to a
picnic in the park. It is important for him to see that you have a
life outside of class too.

6. *Don't be afraid to compliment your professor.* After all, he is human, and I don't know a single human who does not like a sincere compliment. But remember that this is a person of ideas. Make sure your compliment is sincere, and make it fit the professor's needs. The best compliment you can give to a professor is to let him see that he has stimulated you to think of a new idea or to read a book or to create a piece of writing. Let the professor know. It is important for him to know that he is getting through to someone. That is a basic human desire, to feel that we are meeting someone's need.

There you have it—six simple rules for personalizing your professor. Whether you follow the rules or not, don't forget the purpose. Your whole college experience can be made easier and happier if you can just accept what the coach always told you. "These guys put their pants on one leg at a time just like everybody else."

And with that cliché firmly in your mind, you should find going to class, the subject of the next chapter, a rather pleasant experience.

9

Going to Class

I have a secret—a surefire shortcut to getting the best possible grades with the least amount of effort. How does that sound to you? Are you ready for the one suggestion that is going to make the whole college process a breeze? Are you motivated to read further? Well, close the door so this information won't leak out because I am about to reveal an ancient family secret for getting through your classes. Here it is. If you want to survive in the academic world, go to class.

Again, I assure you that I am serious. The first place to start toward your goal of doing well in your classes is to make a vow to yourself that you will not cut classes. Notice. I didn't say that you vow to go when it is convenient or when you are feeling well or when there is nothing else to do. If you want to make the academic work easier, you will go to class every time it meets.

You may have your defenses up. You are looking forward to going to college so you can attend the classes. You won't ever cut, and I am just wasting my time bringing this up. Okay! But remember that promise halfway through the second semester. Make sure that commitment is as strong then as it is now. My advice still stands. If you want to get through classes as easily and as successfully as you can, go (even after the newness wears off).

Almost every student I know who has had academic trouble, started his trouble by missing classes. Usually, if you skip a class, it will take you twice as much time as the class period to make up what you missed. You may as well go in the first place and take the shortcut.

Reasons for Attending Classes

Going to class makes sense for three reasons:

1. Economics. With the rate of tuition we charge at our college, the student pays about seven dollars for each class period in the semester. To miss one of those periods is to blow seven dollars. Have you ever bought a seven-dollar ticket to a movie and not used it? Of course not. You are too frugal for that. So why pay for class periods you don't use. Get your money's worth. Go.

2. Education. You may even be surprised that you can learn something by going to class. In some classes, that is more obvious than in others; but regardless of the amount of material you think is being covered, there is something worthwhile happening in every class session. When you go to class, you are scheduling a part of your day to think about that course. You are learning the language and the structure of that discipline. You are learning how the professor thinks—what is important to him and what his biases are. You are learning how he views things so you can do a better job of anticipating what will be on the test.

3. Public Relations. You also impress the professor when you show up every day. Don't be deceived. Regardless of how big the class is or how aloof the professor may seem, he will remember your face if it is there every day. You will make an impression on him simply by being present, and you will never know when that impression might be of value to you. You may think professors don't care, but they do. As a professor, I take every absence as a personal insult to me and my teaching ability. If you insult me often enough, I will lose confidence in you.

In fact, you may even want to enhance that impression. Develop some facial expressions that you can use as interaction with the professor's ideas. Look as if you are still alive. Smile, nod, frown. All these gestures are unconsciously, if not consciously, recorded and appreciated in the professor's mind. Last semester I had a student in class who nodded his approval of any idea he found significant. I liked the guy. I found myself focusing on him while I talked. I will never forget him because he knew how to make his attendance count for something.

What to Do in Class

So what do you do once you get to class? Well, you have three choices: You can listen; or you can take notes; or, if you are mentally agile, you can listen and take notes at the same time. If you are not coordinated enough to do both, I prefer listening over taking notes; but some professors favor note taking. In fact, someone once defined a college lecture as the process by which notes got transferred from the professor's book to the students' books without passing through the head of either. Your choice here depends on the kind of student you are.

Since lecture is the predominant method of instruction, note taking becomes a valuable art. (In the medieval university, it was such a critical activity that the pope was forced to rule on how fast the professors could lecture.) Every student I know who has thrived in college developed his own style for taking and organizing his notes. Of course, the secret is to develop your own system which recognizes the kind of listener and student you are, but you might profit from some examples.

Systems for Note Taking

1. Buy an individual notebook for each class. Thus, you keep all notes for a particular class together. This is probably the most convenient way to keep notes, but if you have several classes during the day, it means carrying bulky notebooks around.

2. Take notes on a clipboard or yellow pad. Then when you get back to your room, organize the notes for the class period and type the organized and corrected version. This is a good learning situation. You pick up the material in class, and then you review it while it is still current. To make this work, you have to keep up with the organizing and typing. This is probably the most effective system, but it does take time while you are doing it. However, it might actually save you some time, later, during finals week.

3. Share notes with classmates. I recommend this highly for courses where the lecture is important. Get acquainted with some fellow students and swap. Xeroxing is cheap so you both can have each other's notes at the same time. This way, you may get information that you missed. In graduate school, I exchanged notes with a colleague with whom I had several important classes. Recently I reviewed the two sets of notes, and it was difficult to believe that we had been in the same class. Both of us missed some valuable points, but together we had an excellent set of notes.

4. My personal system consisted of organizing my paper. I extend the left-hand margin to a third of the sheet. I then write all the notes on the right two-thirds. Later, when I discover the organizational scheme and outline, I put that in the left-hand third.

I. Go to class *Going to class is easy*

   A. Economics *Get your money's worth*

   B. Education *Learn something*

   C. Public Relations *Please professor*

II. Activities in class

   A. Listen *Listen*

   B. Taking notes *Take notes*

   C. Both *Take notes and listen*

III. Note-taking systems *Systems of note taking*

   A. Several notebooks *several notebooks*

   B. Retype each day *retype*

   C. Share *share*

   D. Split page *split page*

Again, these are only examples of systems. If you adapt one of these, you will have to modify it to fit your own personal style. However, I do have some suggestions to help you develop your own system:

1. Watch for the organization. Almost every body of material, written or oral, has some outline to it. Your ability to take good notes depends on your ability to catch on to the organizational scheme. Some professors are quite good at helping you. They will put an outline on the board or even give you a handout. Others think *you* should do the work. If you need practice in outlining oral presentations, you can start on the minister's sermons or speeches on the radio. But learn to take notes in outline form.

2. Learn to distinguish between facts and concepts. If you have to miss a point, make sure you at least have the concepts.

3. Forget the high school myth that if it is important he will put it on the board. Or that if he puts it on the board it is important. I don't know why other college professors write on the board, but personally, I doodle there.

4. Realize that every discipline has a specific language and structure. If the professor is using terms you don't know, go home and look them up. You won't be much of a listener until you learn the language.

5. If the professor is going too fast, slow him down. The most effective way to do this is to hold up your hand and ask a sensible question about some idea he is discussing. If you can't think that fast, come to class prepared. Actually, most professors will enjoy having a break in the lecture as much as the students will.

If you are still having trouble, you might try going to bed earlier the night before or ingesting a shot of caffeine just before class.

I do hope you find this information on note taking worthwhile, but I present it with some fear. I don't want to present too much material here and cause you to forget the original point of this chapter. If you want to simplify your college classwork and get the best grades with the least possible effort, go to class. It is tough to take notes when you aren't there.

Now that you have been to class, you have recorded all the notes, and listed all the reading assignments, it is time to study. And that's the subject of the next chapter.

10

Studying

Studying is not really a painful activity, but dreading to study is. I offer no tricks or shortcuts here. Effective studying is a matter of discipline. It is the process of deciding that you are going to do it, sitting down, and getting it done; and the sooner you get it over with, the more time you will have free from the dread and the anxiety of knowing you have to study. For some people, studying is even a pleasure, once the good habits are established.

Individual studying should be one of the most time-consuming activities in college. In high school, you spent a major block of time in class. In college, about fifteen hours per week is the average, but you are expected to make up the difference by studying on your own. The traditional advice suggests that you study two hours for every hour you are in class. In some courses, you won't need that much study time, but others will make up for it; so two hours per one hour should be a good guide.

Time Budgets

Since studying does occupy a major portion of your time, I have chosen this spot in the book to talk about time budgets. Believe it or not, there is enough time in college to get everything in, but you have to do some planning—you may have to make a budget. I have observed that college students who don't manage their time wisely lose control of other parts of their lives as well. This time budget is one of the keys to your survival.

Every well-balanced life allows time for three activities: (1) work, which includes going to class, studying, and going to a part-time job if you have one; (2) rest, which means putting your body horizontal and closing your eyes; and (3) recreation, which includes unorganized diversion from stress (such as watching TV, chatting with friends, or staring into space), exercise, and extracurricular activities.

If you are going to make the most of the college experience, you need to build a time schedule that will let you do all of these. I suppose I should break this up into actual hours or percentages, but I don't think that would be helpful because every person is different. I don't know how much sleep you need, but your body knows; and if you don't get as much as your body demands, you are going to cheat everything else you do. If your body demands eight hours of sleep per day, get eight hours. (I find one of the nice things about the college schedule, particularly in this area, is flexibility. I personally need about six hours of sleep each day, so I sleep five hours at night and one hour in the afternoon.)

Some people have greater extracurricular demands; others need more study time. But we all must learn to make the best use of what time we do spend on a project. I am never impressed when someone tells me he spent eight hours studying for an exam. I need to know how profitable the eight hours were. Did he learn anything? Did he retain anything?

That is why you need your own budget. You need to analyze your own time demands and then develop a schedule that includes time for everything—sleep, studying, and even exercise. There is time to get everything in if you just budget it.

The big culprit here is that unorganized diversion from stress. Everybody needs some of this, but if you don't control it, you will find it eating into everything else on your schedule. It is easy to slip into patterns. You sit in the dining hall after the meal for a few minutes to let the food settle, and suddenly you are spending an hour a day there. One recreational game of pool a day explodes into three or four hours in the student union. Your conversations with friends eat into your sleep time.

The solution to this is actually very simple. You can make a time budget and stick rather closely to the time you have allowed for this kind of diversion.

Discipline and the Study Load

Once you have learned to manage your time, you are well on the road to mastering the college study load. From here, it is just a matter of discipline—sitting down and getting to it. I do have some suggestions that might help you develop your own techniques and discipline. Some of these suggestions are just personal hints, but some of them are actually warnings. The college study load may be abruptly different from what you were used to in high school. Anticipating this could save you a teary pillowcase.

1. Don't get behind at the start. (If I repeat this it will sound as if I am emphasizing this warning, so I'll repeat it.) Don't get behind at the start.

Perhaps the biggest difference between high school and college is the difference between the long range and the immediate. In most high school courses, your homework was assigned on a day-by-day basis, and your teacher kept a rather close account of how you were progressing each day.

In college, the assignments, goals, and evaluation periods are more long-range. In some classes you may have no more than one or two tests in an entire sixteen-week period. The rest of the semester, you are on your own to prepare for those tests. The professors will give the reading assignments, but they don't check to see whether you have done them.

This could become a trap. You get the idea that nothing is urgent, so you can afford to play early in the semester. Soon you find yourself behind. To avoid this, start early and study every day of the semester, regardless of what seems to be or not be pressing.

2. *Develop a routine.* Usually the human mind functions best when it is in a familiar setting. To accommodate that little idiosyncrasy, find a regular place and time to put your mind to work. Your choice is a personal one, depending on your own habits and personality; but the important thing is to develop a routine. If you are more effective early in the morning, get up every morning for a study period. If you like to study in close places, put your desk in a corner. If you like quiet and find the dorm noisy, go to the library, but try to sit at the same table each time.

I realize I am strange; but when I was in college, I developed a habit of wearing a hat when I studied. I even bought some beauties especially for that purpose. After all these years, I still haven't broken that habit, but now I am into batting helmets. While I write this, I am wearing the red and white of the Philadelphia Phillies. Just part of my routine.

Recently a man told me that he increased his grade point average by 10 percent when he learned to study for a test in the actual room and seat where he would be taking the test. In other words, when an exam was approaching, he would go to that classroom, turn on the lights, and sit there and study.

This makes sense to me because the mind works best when there is a routine. You may have to discipline yourself, but find a pattern for your study, a routine. Start early and study every day.

3. *Get your exercise.* Earlier, I talked about the value of sleep. Here, I want to remind you of the value of regular exercise to your academic success. When the Romans talked about a sound mind in a sound body, they knew something about learning. Vigorous exercise stimulates creative and intellectual ability. If you don't believe it, try it. Schedule regular sessions for jogging, swimming, playing tennis, weight lifting, or whatever you find invigorating. You don't need to overdo this, but a daily session of vigorous exercise will improve your ability to study. Also, while we are on the physical suggestions, overeating dulls the mind. If you have a big exam coming up tomorrow, you may want to go light on dinner.

4. Take breaks. Don't study past your attention span. If you find your mind wandering, put the books down and take a ten-minute break. Most authorities suggest a ten-minute break every hour. Of course, you may find a need for discipline to get back when the ten minutes are up, particularly when the break coincides with the first ten minutes of "M*A*S*H."

5. Don't put off assignments and force yourself into pressure situations. This may be a restatement of the first point, but too often a student will put off doing something like a term paper. He then forces himself to deal with an impending deadline. Not only is he under pressure but the quality of his work suffers.

6. Be thorough the first time through. As you keep up with your readings, make good notes. Outline all the pertinent information. Write down all the data in an organized form. This will save you precious time and anxiety during test week.

7. Have all study sources close at hand. Get in the habit of keeping a good supply of paper, pens, and colored pencils around. Have a good dictionary, thesaurus, and necessary reference books where you can get at them. Popping up to get something you've forgotten can erase everything you have been learning.

8. Learn to use the library. I make this statement boldly, although I hope you don't need it. Unfortunately, too many college students do. You would be amazed at the number of students who tell me that they never went into the library the first two years they were on campus. That is sad. The library is your friend. Get acquainted with it during the first week you are in college. Go in; check things out; see what is available. If you can't find something, ask a librarian. If you don't know how to use a piece of equipment (computer, microfiche reader) ask a librarian. Those people are paid from your tuition money. They are there to help you. Help them earn their salaries.

I know you think I am overstressing this point; but if you will get acquainted with the library during your first week and make a habit of using it, you will thank me someday.

9. Study with a colleague. If you have done your homework, if you have read all the assignments and reviewed your notes, your "Let's get together and study for the test" friend can be a great asset. You can help fill the gaps in each other's knowledge, offer two perspectives, drill each other, and break the loneliness of studying alone.

10. Realize why you are studying. I have saved the best for last. I want to close on a positive note. Through the reading of this list, you might infer that studying is a boring obligation with the only purpose of helping you pass. But I want to leave you with the exact opposite idea. Studying is necessary to make the grades, and you have to make certain grade level in order to graduate. But studying is far more important to you than that. Studying is a liberating process, the process by which you learn more about yourself and the world you live in. Through those meaningful hours of study, you will unlock some of the mysteries of the universe, of other people, of the routes of human history, of your own body and soul. And if you look through these mysteries, you will recognize a unifying Spirit that gives all things order and meaning. Look forward to your opportunity to pore through the books, to write the papers, to work the problems. You will be a fuller person because of it, and life will take on a new quality. You may even catch a glimpse of the glory of God.

A Matter of Discipline

Although these suggestions may not make your study load easier, they should help you become more effective in using your time. It is still a matter of discipline, and I can't give you that—only a reminder. Don't forget that commencement scene in the preface. Most of those happy graduates became graduates because they learned to study. Very few people make it through college on native ability. They all learn to study. So can you if the motivation is great enough.

Since reading and writing are the two most common skills used in studying, I will discuss these in the next two chapters.

11

Reading

Next to listening, reading is the most valuable skill in college academics. Whether you want to or not, whether you consider yourself good at it or not, you will spend several hours reading before you earn the right to hug everybody at commencement.

You may as well decide that you like it. You may as well learn to enjoy it. And if you are not very good at it, you may as well work at improving yourself. You are going to need the skill.

In fact, be cautious of anybody who offers you miraculous shortcuts. There are ways to improve your reading skills, and there are some methods for improving your speed. But scholarship is still a lonely, slow, and sometimes tedious process. Being well informed, well educated, well read demands time. You just have to realize that the results are worth the efforts; then you have to commit yourself to the time it takes to become well educated.

Frequently, students tell me that they are slow readers, and I suspect that some of them really are slower than others. But mostly what they are telling me is, "I don't want to spend the time reading." I don't offer any sympathy, but I do have one piece of advice: If you are a slow reader, buy a comfortable cushion for your chair.

Improving Your Reading

Although I can't tell you how to speed up the process, I do have some suggestions that might help you become a more effective reader, particularly of college textbooks.

1. Read each discipline differently. Each course you take has a distinctive language and structure. The books for those courses reflect those distinctions. If you are going to comprehend a textbook, you have to understand something about the field before you start. The more you understand about the field, the easier the book will be to read.

My field is educational philosophy. When educational philosophers write a book, they have a certain style; they refer to certain people; they use specialized terms. Because I know all about this, I breeze right through educational philosophy. On the other hand, you ought to see me tackle a chemistry book.

Actually, one of the purposes for taking a course is to learn how to read the material. If you take my course, I would want you to learn how to read educational philosophy. If you take a course in romantic poetry, you should learn how to read romantic poetry. If you take a course in math, you should learn how to read math language.

You can get a head start on some of this by preparing yourself before you jump feetfirst into that forty-dollar textbook big enough to give you a hernia if you carry it too far. Check the bookstore or the library to see if you can find an outline series for the course. Read any of this kind of material you can find. These outlines are not designed to substitute for the reading, but they can help you understand what you are about to read. The reading itself will be so much more productive.

Also, check the textbook thoroughly before you begin reading. Look over the table of contents and the sequence of units. Read the preface and dedication notes. If there is a glossary or index at the end, read it before you begin.

Then as you start reading, look for the key names and terms which will help you understand the field. If you don't recognize the references, make an appointment and go ask the professor. (I made that suggestion earlier, so I just repeat it in this context.)

This can be summarized in one important point: Each discipline reads differently from any other discipline. Recognize those differences as you are reading.

2. Read with a purpose. Reading is like any other hunt-and-seek game. You can play it better if you know what you are looking for. It really helps the effectiveness of your reading to know what you are looking for before you begin to read.

If the professor has given any questions or suggestions, use those. If not, look for questions at the end of the chapter. Many authors insert those for your benefit. Read them before you start so you will know what the author thought he was saying.

If you have no questions available, at least survey the total assignment before you begin, noting headings, pictures, diagrams, and so on. And this leads us to point 3.

3. For good results, survey first, read, and then review. You probably heard of this process when you were in elementary school, but it is also effective at the college level. (The dean tells me that he sees a lot of elementary behavior at the college level.)

4. Find the organizational scheme. This point may remind you of a similar suggestion in the chapter on note taking. The advice and the procedure are the same. Every author writes with some scheme of organization. Every author also develops some kind of pattern of construction. If you can find that scheme and pattern, you can get more out of the reading and take notes that will help you in the review.

For example, look for major points and support points. Look for topic sentences in each paragraph and mark them for future reference. If you find an organizational scheme, make notes either in the margin or in a notebook. (I prefer the margin because I sometimes have setting recall. In other words, I can remember where the statement was on the page. That's a handy little skill at test time.)

Today, one of my colleagues handed me an article that he had just spent more than an hour reading. He asked me to read it and discuss it with him. I read it in ten minutes, and during the discussion, I realized that we had both remembered about the same from the article. Why? Am I that much better a reader than he? Of course not. But when he read the article, he had graciously marked the topic sentence of every paragraph with a yellow outlining pen. I just read his outline. This kind of thorough reading and marking can really help you when you need to review the material for the exam.

5. *Read with a dictionary nearby.* This point will be repeated in nearly every chapter in the book, but it is still important. Use the dictionary. Get out of that bad habit of skipping over words you don't know. Those words were carefully chosen by the author to communicate something. Find out what.

6. *Set realistic goals for each sitting.* Edgar Allan Poe thought that a good story could be read in one sitting, but don't try that with *War and Peace.* The mind is like any other sponge. When it gets full, it won't soak up anything until it dries out. Set a goal before you start to read, but don't read beyond your saturation point.

7. *Personalize the author.* (Does this remind you of an earlier chapter?) Books are written by people. People are human. They have likes and dislikes, aches and pains, strengths and weaknesses. They sometimes do things well and sometimes make mistakes. The written word is not infallible. You don't have to agree with or accept everything in the book. To disagree with a book is the same as having a friendly argument with your roommate. It is simply a disagreement with another human.

Now that I have convinced you of this, let me convince you to find out everything you can about that human who wrote your book. Read the preface and introduction. Look him up in the biographical dictionary, encyclopedia, or journal index. Get acquainted with this human.

8. Interact with the material. Reading is an active process. As you read bring your own emotions, ideas, and opinions to the material. Don't be in such a hurry to get through the page that you can't allow yourself time to evaluate what you have received through reading.

9. Take time for recreational and devotional reading. There is an old joke about postmen who take walks on their holidays, and here I am suggesting to college students who read all day to take a break and do some reading. But you do need to remember how to read for entertainment. You need to read material that you won't be tested on—material that will make you happy or sad but won't need to be remembered for an exam. Depending on your taste, keep something like a sports magazine, a light romance, comics, or a whodunit around to give you a break from the stuff you have to read.

Also, don't forget your devotional life. Schedule some time each day to read material that will address your personal needs, offer advice, encourage you, and give you confidence and direction. For this, I recommend the Bible. It has material for every mood, and it offers enlightenment and encouragement. Besides, reading the Bible may help you evaluate and understand some of the textbooks you are trying to master.

The Privilege of Reading

Reading is a fulfilling privilege. Going to college where the reading is organized and directed is a particular privilege.

You should look forward to the great things you are going to discover in books during your college career. The hunt will require many hours, regardless of how fast you read, but in the words of Sir Francis Bacon, sixteenth-century English scholar and scientist, it will make you a full person. And that is why you are going to college in the first place—to become a more complete human being.

12

Writing

After you have become full of knowledge from all your read-ing, you will need to learn to be precise with what you know. That is the purpose of writing. (Bacon said that writing makes one exact.)

The opportunity to write is also a privilege. It gives you a chance to organize your thoughts, to see how things relate, and to see which ideas can stand the test of written expression. Writing is communication between you and the teacher. It is your oppor-tunity to tell the professor what you think of the ideas, what you think is important enough to remember, and how you can apply the ideas to your situation.

One of the things you should look forward to in a college edu-cation is the opportunity to perfect your skills of organization, idea development, and written communication. This is one of the purposes of going to college. When you graduate, you will take your place among the educated of the world, and those are the people who are shaping things with the written word. In college, you will learn how to be a part of that.

Making It Easier

However, if you are anticipating those writing assignments and opportunities with something less than great enthusiasm, perhaps I can help you alleviate some of the fears and reservations by making several points about the nature of the college writing experience. Some of these points are descriptive; some are prescriptive. If you are already a good writer (in other words, if you like to write and you do it well), you may not need the prescriptive remarks. Writing is a matter of personal style, so I don't propose to force you into a mold. Nevertheless, you may want to save this chapter for future reference should you lose your confidence as a writer at any time during your college experience.

1. "Word block" is a reality. For years, educators have accepted the psychological barrier called math block. Some people become so frightened by figures that their minds don't function properly. This same thing happens to some people with writing assignments. This is a rather severe problem, so you may not have it. But if you do, you may want to practice. Tell someone your favorite ghost story or joke. Then write it out word for word as you told it. Working from a familiar text will help you overcome the fear. After all, writing is just recorded talking.

2. Usually, college writing assignments fall into one of three categories. These are research writing, the position paper, and the essay test. Although all these activities are similar, there are some differences, and you need to make allowances for those differences. The research paper is a report. It emphasizes the factual. The position paper is usually more persuasive. Thus, it requires a different kind of language and structure. The essay test may be like one of the first two, or it may be a combination of both; but it almost always has the added dimension of a time restriction. (How does your hand feel after two hours of solid scribbling?)

Of course, there are courses in writing (creative writing, journalism, and so on) that provide exceptions to these three categories, but in these courses the assignment is more specific by its own nature.

3. The purpose of doing a research paper is the research. Often college students dread the research paper because they consider it another writing assignment. But this is the wrong attitude. Students frequently complain that college courses are too broad; professors cover too much material in too short a time; students don't have time to study anything in depth. Well, the research paper offers you the chance to correct that. If you do a good job of selecting and narrowing the topic of your research paper, you can spend weeks in the library digging out all sorts of interesting material. You can take the time to study one minute point in detail. Who knows? You may become the world's foremost expert on that one point.

If you look at the project as an opportunity to do research, and if you are thorough in that research, writing the paper will be easy.

Of course, every professor wants you to follow the "proper" form for documentation (footnotes and bibliography), and there are about as many proper forms of documentation as there are varieties of breakfast cereal. You will have to find out what he wants. The best way to do this is to borrow a paper from one of his former students and see what style was used. (This is a professional hint. Those of us who write research articles for journals always use an article from that journal as a model.)

4. In writing, organization is the key factor. Knowing how to organize your thoughts will not only make the assignment easier and faster, it will also help you eliminate your fears and dreads. Everybody who is well organized is organized around a system. If you don't have a system of your own for organizing your ideas, let me propose mine. It has been rather effective for me, both in speaking and in writing. It helps me get to the ideas quickly, and it helps me edit out what I can't use.

When you first get an assignment, *jot down everything you know about the topic.* (On research papers, this jotting will take place after you have done all the research.) Don't worry about structure and form. Just get the ideas down. (Be sure to use this on an essay exam. If you jot down all the ideas and information first, you won't forget an idea when you get into the pressure of writing. When professors give an essay question, they are looking for certain points. The more of these you can remember and mention, the better your performance.)

When you have completed your jot-down outline, *pick out a few general points from it.* (I always use three points here because I have been programmed by listening to three-point sermons.) Use those general points as the major points in your outline. Then categorize all the other points under the appropriate main point. If something doesn't fit, throw it away. One of the merits of this system is that it helps you edit out what you can't use.

Actually, everything I have said can be summarized in one statement: *Outline before you start.* If you prepare an outline that tells you where you are going, you will save a lot of time getting there. If you have never learned to outline before you begin to write, I urge you—I implore you—get in the habit. If you do, you will love me for the suggestion and your professors will love me. (Yours may be another hug I get on graduation day.)

5. *Now that you have points, you need to develop them.* Again, I offer you my system. If you have one that works for you, good. If not, consider mine. You can modify it if you want.

The first task is to state the point. In bold, positive language— *state your point.* And do it at the beginning. If I am reading your essay test, I don't want to search for the topic sentence. I want it in plain sight.

Next, *explain the point.* Offer a few sentences of general explanation.

Then, *illustrate the point.* This is important. Most of us remember the illustrations long after we have forgotten the explanation. Most of us remember the points because we remember the illustrations. For a lesson in illustration techniques, read some of the philosophical works of C. S. Lewis. He makes deep points simple because of his ability to use common illustrations.

What are good illustrations? They are such things as jokes, personal stories, statistics, direct and indirect quotations from literature. (In fact, this is the most important thing to remember when taking a literature essay test. Document your points by mentioning specific passages from the works themselves.)

Finally, after you have stated the point, explained it, and illustrated it, *restate the point.* Make one final, summarizing, closing statement. You are now ready to go to the next point.

If you are not positive and enthusiastic about your writing, this explanation for developing a point could be invaluable to you. It provides direction—you know where you are going before you even start—and it provides a formula for getting your ideas across.

6. *Construction is a matter of common sense and using the resources.* If you are a high school graduate, you know enough about construction skills to be an effective writer. Your task is to use what you know. Most correctness is the result of common sense. Use sentences that you can analyze and punctuate. If you don't know how to punctuate it, rewrite it in your own language. Use words you know. The purpose of good writing is effective communication. If being fancy helps you communicate, be fancy; but if it gets in your way, be simple.

Of course, you will need to acquire and learn to use certain writing resources such as a good dictionary (it is inexcusable to hand in a paper with a misspelled word), a thesaurus (for when you have word block), and a grammar handbook (no one expects you to remember all those rules for capital letters, punctuation, and subject–verb agreement; but you should know where to find the rules).

7. *Learn to type.* After being around colleges for a major portion of my life, I have decided that the four most essential skills for academic success are listening, reading, writing, and typing. If you don't know how to type, give yourself some quicky lessons in your spare time before you get to college. Typing is not a difficult skill. I mastered it, and you ought to see my tennis game.

Being able to type will save you frustration, time, and money during your college career. Besides, the computer keyboards are becoming so popular that you may someday need the skill just to order lunch. (You think I exaggerate? Already in a local library, you have to know how to type to check out a book.)

8. Learn to compose at the typewriter. Composing your papers at the typewriter is a learned skill, which could not only save you time but could help you be more effective in your writing. Typing allows you to look off into space as you think and put your thoughts into words. It also gives your fingers a better chance of keeping up with your mind.

At this point, you don't want to worry too much about making a beautiful, error-free copy. You can always rewrite.

If you don't already compose at the typewriter, I suggest you give it a try just for practice. Sit down and put together an essay. Force yourself to learn to do composing. It is a skill worth developing.

Overcoming Fears and Dreads

I hope these descriptive and prescriptive points help you understand the purpose and nature of college writing, and I hope that by understanding you can overcome whatever fears and dreads you may have. It is actually through the experience of writing that you will begin to understand yourself a little better—you will begin to comprehend the meaning of your own fingerprints. And who knows? You may like writing and thinking so well that you become an author. It happened to one person I know.

13

Handling the Ideas

College is a place of ideas. The people who work at colleges work with their minds, and ideas are the products of mind work. The books you read are records of those ideas. Some of those ideas are very good—sound, forceful, valuable. Some are not so valuable or even sound. But they are all floating around the college campus.

I have saved this reminder as the conclusion to this section on academics. All your listening, reading, and writing are centered around the nature and purpose of good and bad ideas. Both kinds exist, regardless of where you go to college. I give you this information to prepare you for what you will encounter. I want you to know that you will be exposed to many ideas. Some will be unusual and controversial.

I don't have much patience with those students who run in to tell the dean that their professor is thinking. Sure he is thinking. That is what he is getting paid to do. It shouldn't come as any surprise.

If you rushed to this chapter because you want me to tell you how to prevent your professors from saying anything you don't agree with, I apologize. You won't get any of that from me. Even if I knew how to prevent professors from thinking and saying what they thought about (and I don't), I wouldn't tell you. You are a college student now. It is time for you to learn to handle ideas on your own.

The Measuring Stick

Ideas are not to be suppressed or forbidden or rejected or even accepted. They are to be considered, analyzed, researched, criticized, and evaluated. But in order to evaluate them, you need a measuring stick, and you have to bring that to college with you.

When you come to college, you need to bring with you some method for evaluating all the ideas you hear. That method may not be perfect when you first come, but it will get stronger through use. Sure, you are going to be exposed to a variety of ideas. Some of them will become a permanent part of you; but some of them, after consideration, will be rejected. That is part of the process of intellectual growth. Your task is to decide how you are going to screen ideas. What are you going to use to make a judgment about what ideas you will accept and which ones you will reject?

This is actually a very important task. An idea is a rather powerful tool in the world and in an individual's life. Actually, an idea is like an egg. If you leave it in a warm, dry place, it will hatch into something alive—an action. So your actions during the rest of your life will originate from ideas. And some of those ideas will become a part of you during the four years you are in college—during those four years when you grow from an adolescent to an adult, during those four years when you modify some of your belief structure. Before you get into that process, you need to develop a measuring stick by which you can evaluate those powerful agents called ideas.

Where do you get that measuring stick? You build it from a combination of your past and your future. Based on what you have been taught and what you have discovered about life combined with what you want life to be like after you have finished college, you develop a technique for evaluating ideas.

A good evaluation tool will develop through use. In other words, if you have a good procedure for evaluating the information and ideas you encounter through listening and reading, you will not only grow intellectually but you will also grow in your ability to assess the value and foresee the consequences of an idea. You will begin to see what an idea might mean if it were put into practice.

The easiest way for me to explain the way this procedure of evaluation works is for me to explain my own measuring stick. I submit this to show you the mechanics of how such a system works. I have developed it from my own background and my own aspirations, so it suits me. If you are going to be effective in handling new and perhaps unusual ideas, you will need to develop your own. You may, however, borrow from mine if you wish.

1. Is this idea biblically sound? (This is the first question I ask.) Does this idea contradict a clear, certain biblical principle?

Originally I asked this question because I had been taught that the Bible should be used as a test of truth. I still believe that, but now I believe it more emphatically. In recent years, I have come to believe that the Bible represents the wisest piece of advice for human living that I can find. If I can follow the principles of the Bible and stay within the framework of its teaching, life will be simpler, more effective, and more fun. So I ask first, "Is this idea biblically sound?"

Of course, to answer this question, I must know something about the Bible. In fact, I need a growing knowledge of the Bible. I must study. If you want to use the Bible as a test of the validity of an idea, then you must have a thorough and growing knowledge of what the Bible says. Thus, the Bible becomes an important sourcebook for all of your college studies.

2. Is this idea usable and practical in the world of human affairs? Since I am an educational philosopher, nearly everybody I meet and everything I read outlines some principle for making schools run better. They are all great ideas, products of good minds. Unfortunately, some of them are totally impractical. The thinkers have overlooked some point of reality which makes the idea unworkable. I need to know if such a point has been overlooked before I jump in and endorse any idea. I need to know if the idea is usable in the real world

3. What will be the outcome of this idea if it is implemented? This question is based on the answer to question 2. Before I accept an idea and catalog it among my personal beliefs and doctrines, I need to know what it means to people. Will it do the greatest amount of good to the greatest number, or is it primarily a selfish idea designed to help a chosen few?

To make this decision, it helps to have some sense of history. Frequently, we hear what seems to be a new idea only to find out that it failed at an earlier time.

4. Is this idea personally satisfying? Frankly, I believe some of what I believe because I want to. For example, as an educational philosopher, I tend to endorse a more traditional view of the schooling process than some of my colleagues. But I find my position completely satisfying. I am glad I believe that. The belief solves a lot of personal problems for me.

By the same logic, you would be less than honest to deny that many of your beliefs are chosen simply because they fit your personality and your personal needs. However, I submit this with some reservation. This is just one test in a whole scheme for evaluating ideas. If you are not careful, this can become the only test; then you will have denied yourself your right to grow intellectually, and that contradicts the purpose of the college experience.

Professors and Ideas

Now that you have developed your system for evaluating ideas and you are prepared for the onslaught, you are ready to go to class. Once there, you may find two kinds of professors: those who present ideas as ideas and those who present ideas as facts. You need to learn the difference between these two quickly.

If the professor is presenting ideas as ideas, he is looking for interaction. He is trying to help you perfect your measuring stick by providing you with the material. To do well in this class you will need the ability to evaluate, defend, and develop based on the evidence presented.

But you will be free to accept or reject any idea you choose. Of course, this freedom may cause you some pain until you get used to it. Too often, we like to have people tell us what to believe.

On the other hand, some professors present ideas as if they are facts. They are looking for acceptance. In such classes, you have three choices. You can accept the ideas, and they will become a part of you, or you can reject the ideas personally, but keep your rejection to yourself. You can play the game, take the notes, answer the test questions as the professor likes, and escape with the grade and (I hope) your basic beliefs intact.

Or, you can reject the ideas and make an issue of your rejection. This, of course, is honest. You have defended a personal freedom—the freedom to think. If you choose this route, I recommend that you be tactful and personal. Go to the professor and meet with him one to one. Don't let the difference between you become a hindrance to the tone of the class. He has as much right to teach his ideas as you have to express yours.

In the midst of all this, you need to remember the educational value of the exchange of ideas, regardless of the professor's attitude toward it. I am not proposing that you be so open-minded that you are in danger of your brain falling out, but I am proposing that you have your own measuring stick so finely tuned that you can be challenged by an idea but not corrupted by it.

When we talk of controversial ideas among college professors, the discussion usually centers around two general areas: political and economical theories and theories about the origin of the universe. Since you have already been exposed to those discussions and you have some of your own ideas regarding them, I would rather provide you with an opportunity to practice your evaluation system on another example of a potentially dangerous idea rampant on college campuses. This kind of idea, in fact, may be more dangerous than the others because nobody is talking about it. Consider the following example.

Definition of success. Sometime during your life, you are going to make a decision about what the good life is. You are going to decide what you must do in order to feel that your life has been successful.

At college, you will encounter several influences to help you with that decision, and those influences represent ideas. Unfortunately, some of those ideas can be dangerous because they could limit you as a person. It is quite possible that you could emerge from four years of college with the very limited definition of success—that which says that to be successful you must be among the leading consumers of the country. In other words, you may emerge from college believing that the only definition of success is having a big house, a fancy car, and the money to buy the pleasures of the world.

If you have measured this idea and have actively chosen it, I don't have any quarrel. But I would hope that your college education would give you an alternative definition of success—that if you choose a profession which does not make you a leading consumer, you can still be happy and feel successful.

I have used this example to show you how your device for evaluating ideas is constantly being applied. Your definition of success is an idea that will hatch into action. If you have not actively selected your definition of success but have only memorized it from all the influences around you, then you have surrendered some of your uniqueness which college should be developing. To prevent this, you need to use your stick for measuring ideas.

A Look Into the World

With this warning, I conclude this section on the academic side of college life. If you are not afraid of yourself, if you are not afraid of the power of your own mind, going to class, reading, writing, and thinking are exciting, entertaining, and rewarding experiences. College classwork can open doors to insights of a bigger, brighter, more exciting world than you have ever imagined. But once the door is open, you have to enter that world on your own initiative.

In other words, college studies can offer you a new look at the world, if you let them.

Part III

THE INSTITUTION

14

Institutions and Bureaucracy

Now you have thought about how to manage your relationship with your roommates, friends, dates, parents, and professors. And you have also thought about how you are going to assimilate and evaluate the information and ideas you encounter in class so that you can become a truly educated person, one who functions in the world of affairs with intellectual soundness and emotional stability. But you still have one lesson to learn. You must learn how to get along with the institution itself.

Every college is an institution. Although some institutions operate better than others, they all have some common features. If you are ever going to achieve any kind of happiness while you are in college, you will need to understand something about the structure of institutions in general and yours in particular.

Not a Person

The first thing you should learn is that an institution is not a person, but that is a difficult lesson to learn. Often students, and occasionally even professors, don't recognize this basic point. You may see people at the institution. They are standing behind counters or seated behind desks where they look important and official. You may see people in such places as the dean's office and even the president's office. But the institution is bigger than

123

any one of these people. In fact, it is bigger than all of them put together. Since the institution is bigger than those people who look important and represent it, it is also bigger than you. The institution is a combination of all the rules and all the officials and all the student interests and all the buildings and all the traditions and legends. It has become what it is through years of development, and it probably won't change a whole lot just because *you* arrived.

It is important that you know this. Don't expect the institution to respond to you as a person. It can't. It is not a person. Those people behind those counters might represent the institution, but they are not the institution. Some of them might even respond to you as a person, but the institution itself can't.

This point still shocks me occasionally. I have colleagues who have given most of their lives to the institution where I teach. Suddenly, after years of devoted service, they die. Well, I want the institution to do something. I want us to stop everything and recognize that we have lost a devoted servant. But institutions can't function that way. People may pause and mourn what we have lost, but the institution must go on.

I tell you this so you won't be shocked or offended the first time the institution treats you in a nonpersonal way. Regardless of where you go to school, the institution is still not a person. It must function as an institution.

For one thing, the institution is more permanent than you are. It was there before you came, and it will probably be there long after you are gone. You may contribute to its legends, but the institution will outlast you.

For another thing, the institution must represent every student it has now, it has had, or it will ever have. Whether you are one out of four hundred or one out of forty thousand (depending on where you go to school), you are still just one student.

In order to deal with all students, the institution must practice the rites of efficiency. Your application for admission, your registration form, your application for financial aid, your housing assignment, your request for special information are all handled as quickly and as easily as possible. If the people who represent the institution spent too much time on you, they wouldn't have time for everyone else. If you can understand this, you might become more tolerant of the people who work for the institution.

Dealing With the Institution

Actually, that is the purpose of this chapter—to suggest that you understand the institution well enough that you don't let the impersonal efficiency and the occasional errors upset you. You can survive these. You just need some patience and a bit of understanding. Let me make some suggestions which may help you with both.

1. Pay attention to announcements. Look! I have been to high schools recently. I know what happens during the reading of the announcements. I have been in high schools where not one single student has heard one single announcement in years. The announcement time is the time to catch up on last night and the next weekend. If you don't hear something important, someone will remind you.

Well, college is different. You must pay attention. Every college has some method for communicating the important announcements—a daily sheet, a special section in the campus newspaper, or even a bulletin board. The first thing you need to learn is how the announcements are communicated. Then you must keep posted. Don't get the attitude that there is never anything for you. Someday there will be; and if you miss out, you have no one to blame except yourself.

2. Remember that people run institutions. Despite my strong speech about the impersonal nature of institutions, those people in charge are still people. As people, they are capable of making mistakes. If people make mistakes, the mistakes can be corrected.

Some people don't enjoy admitting they have made mistakes, but once they have been convinced, their mistakes can be corrected.

The suggestion here is *persist*. If you think you have been treated unfairly, that a mistake has been made, check with the person responsible. Don't boil and fret. Check first.

If your grade is lower than you thought it should be, check with the professor. Don't be argumentative; just check. If a mistake has been made, it will be corrected.

If there is a mistake on your bill, if some department accuses you of not turning in a form you know you did turn in, if you don't get as much financial aid as you thought you would, if you are blamed for something you didn't do, go to the people responsible for sending you the nasty letters and find out if a mistake has been made. Although the institution must operate efficiently, it has no intentions of treating you unjustly. (And if it does make a mistake, don't take it personally. It happens to the best of us.)

3. Go to the person who has the power to make a decision. Everybody must answer to somebody. Even the president of the college himself must answer to the board. If you need to correct an injustice or ask for a special favor, you may need to go through the chain of command until you find that person. Most of those people behind those counters deal with routine questions, so they have routine answers. If the routine answer is sufficient, you are in good shape. If it isn't, go to the next person up until you get the final answer.

4. Get everything in writing. Occasionally, you will ask administrators and advisors to make special decisions about the specifics of your college program. Always get those decisions in writing. I don't mean to imply by this suggestion that the people do not have the integrity to keep their word. They are probably very honest. But they may forget, or even worse, they may disappear.

College officials quit and die. In either case, the man who promised you that you wouldn't need a certain course for graduation may not be around when you graduate three years later.

To make things easy for the official who will make the decision, write a little note explaining exactly what you are requesting. If he grants it, ask him to sign your note. That way you will have a signed record of his agreement.

5. Fill out forms promptly and properly. Remember that the institution must operate efficiently. Do your part to help that efficiency. Cooperate every chance you get. When you help the institution operate efficiently, you have helped it save money. And that money it saves is your tuition money. If the institution saves enough money, maybe it will buy some new tennis nets, and everybody will be happy.

6. Preserve your integrity. That may seem like a strange comment right in the midst of these suggestions about dealing with the institution, but I wanted to get your attention. Let me restate the suggestion. Don't forge names on official documents. Is that blunt enough? If you have never been to college, you may not know what I am talking about; but you will soon enough. When you need an advisor's signature on one more registration form and the line closes in five minutes, you are going to be strongly tempted to go against everything you have ever been taught. Besides, it's two blocks to the professor's office, and he is never there anyway. One signature won't hurt.

But this is a bad practice. Forging names is both illegal and immoral. Don't lose your integrity.

7. Avoid the "they oughter" syndrome. This is a rather common disease that affects most of us at some time. When we are angry, when we have been dealt an injustice, or when we don't like the way things are going, we blame all the trouble on somebody named "They." This kind of indefinite blaming doesn't do much good other than letting you vent your hostility. To get at the issue, find out who is responsible. If you are going to waste a lot of your time criticizing, at least criticize a specific person.

8. Be courteous. Sure you have been cheated. Sure you have been given the runaround. Sure, the other people have been rude to you. I know that. But that still doesn't give you a license to act subhuman. Remember your manners despite the situation. A cheerful smile and an attempt to understand are far more persuasive than a cross word or a threat.

9. Don't let the operation of the institution interfere with your education. I have known students who have been almost consumed by their hatred for the institutional character of the college. Frequently, our conversations go something like this:

"Do you have good teachers?"

"Yes, the teachers are great."

"What about your friends?"

"I have got the greatest bunch of friends a person could have."

"You like the food?"

"Not bad." (No self-respecting college student will ever admit that he likes the food.)

"So what is your complaint?"

"The college made a mistake on my bill."

"Is it that bad?"

"Yes, I hate this place."

This poor student has put far too much emphasis on one mistake. In so doing, he has overlooked all the real reasons he came to college. Unfortunately, he may let this anger fester for years, even after he has graduated. Guard against this kind of attitude. It only hurts you. The institution itself will escape from this anger almost unharmed.

This brings me back to my thesis. The college is an institution. As such, it has bureaucracy, bureaucrats, and bureaucratic mistakes. You need to learn to deal with these. You must learn to follow the proper channels to take care of yourself and your interests, but you shouldn't let the bureaucracy destroy your confidence or your love for the college.

15

Choosing a Major

Yesterday, I counseled two college seniors. One told me that she had wanted to be an elementary school teacher ever since she was six years old. During her childhood she had played school. In high school she was a teacher's aide and president of the Future Teachers' Association. When she got to college, she declared elementary education as her major, and now, four years later, she is only eight weeks away from her lifetime dream.

The other student came to college with no definite plans. After sampling the general education courses, he more or less wandered into a liberal arts major where he did very well. Now with eight weeks left in his entire college career, he has decided that what he really wants to do is become a kindergarten teacher.

Both students have had good college experiences. Both have enjoyed their classes, have grown intellectually and emotionally, have expanded their world view, and have become educated. The only difference is that one chose a major which led to a definite profession while the other didn't.

All this illustrates the thesis of this chapter. Choosing a major is a highly personal matter. In order to make the right choice, you have to know what you want from college, and you have to know the best way to obtain it.

The advice in this chapter is based on the assumption that your primary purpose for coming to college was to become edu-

cated, to learn something about yourself and the universe and
how those two entities can live together effectively; and this purpose should be the dominant consideration in choosing a major.
Despite the career-related tone of some of my suggestions in this
chapter, you will be more likely to thrive in college (actually
enjoy it) if you can keep the professional goals from overshad-
owing the broader educational purpose. In other words, if you
come to college as a premed major, don't let that fact keep you
from participating in and enjoying the aesthetic and social life
around you.

Now that you have your educational purpose in mind, I shall
offer you some help for going through the process of choosing a
major. As you remember these suggestions, remember that some
majors do lead directly to careers, so in many cases a decision to
choose a major course of study in college is basically a professional decision. However, many majors don't lead directly to
career choices. You must decide what is appropriate for you.

What to Know

In order to make an intelligent decision concerning your
major, you need to have an honest and objective evalution of
what you like to study and what you would like to do in life as
well as an understanding of what your college offers. Let's look
at each of these more closely.

1. What do you like to study and what do you want to do in life?
Although some parents disagree with me, I put the question of
what you like to study at the top of the list. College is enough of a
pressure situation as it is. There is no need for you to add to it by
choosing to spend most of your time studying material you don't
enjoy or that is difficult for you. Before you choose a major, ask
yourself, "What do I really enjoy studying?"

If you enjoy numerical logic and problem solving, you may
want to major in math or some area related to math such as engi-

neering or computer science. On the other hand, if you don't enjoy those things, stay out of the math-related majors despite all the reports you have heard about the wide-open job market in computers. If you don't enjoy the study, you won't enjoy the work either; and there is no need to plan a miserable life.

If you enjoy details and numbers, you may want to major in accounting or some area related to accounting such as law or economics. On the other hand ...

If you enjoy studying the past and reading historical material, you may want to major in history or something similar such as archeology, anthropology, or library science (which could lead you into such jobs as an archivist or a museum curator).

If you enjoy reading imaginative and emotional writings, you may want to major in literature, advertising, drama, or creative writing.

I have emphasized the preceding point intentionally. I want you to spend some time thinking about what you really enjoy studying and how your mind works. But I also want you to spend some time investigating all the career possibilities that each college major offers. Unfortunately, most of us don't do enough of this kind of investigation. Too often, young people believe that one comes to college to learn to be a doctor or a lawyer or a school teacher, so they don't explore the thousands of other career choices available to them. Because of this limited view of professional choices, too many of them do not make sound decisions about majors.

Before you get to college, spend some time investigating the wide world of career choices; then decide how what you enjoy studying fits into one of these professions, if it does at all.

If your major doesn't seem to be leading to any particular career option, don't despair. Remember that going to college has an educational purpose first and a professional purpose second.

2. What does your college offer? If you have a lifelong burning desire to study a particular field, you probably took this into consideration when you went through the process of choosing a college. Since that is the topic of the next chapter, I will save the discussion until then.

If, however, you have found yourself in a certain college with no particular major in mind, you may want to do some research before you declare something definite. I have some hints for that research.

A. *Develop a good system for evaluating a specific department.* Frequently, students are encouraged to ask, "Is this the best department and best major on campus?" But this may be a misleading question. A better question might be, "If I were going to major in this particular discipline, where should I go to college?" This prevents comparing apples and oranges. (What kind of a question is, "Is the P.E. department better than the philosophy department?" What are we going to use to measure the two to make the comparison?)

B. *Read the catalog.* Find out what is required and what is covered in each class. Check the credentials of the professors. See how many options you have.

C. *Make your own decision.* Be careful of following the crowd to the most popular department. Find a place where you fit in.

D. *Get acquainted with the professors.* Attend orientation openhouses. Sample some courses. Go to open lectures conducted by professors from various departments. See what each department has to offer.

A Summary

Now that you have an honest evaluation of what you want to study and your educational needs, and you have made some investigation of the various departments on campus, you are ready to start the sometimes painful process of choosing your major. To assist you with the decision, I have, as a summary, a list of reminders that you will want to consider as you make the decision.

1. Some majors lead directly to career choices; some do not. If you are in a hurry to get out into a specific profession or if you are in a hurry to get into a professional graduate program (such as law or medicine), your choice of major may be fairly limited. On the other hand, if the career choice is not that obvious, you have some options.

2. Don't be afraid to change majors. Most college students do. (I would give you the statistics of what percentage do switch majors, but it changes with each generation of students.) Don't be afraid or embarrassed if you decide after a couple of years that you have a stronger interest in another field. Also, don't let your advisor pressure you. You have a right to change majors. If you are moving out of a small department, your advisor may not want you to go. But make the decision yourself. The department will survive your leaving.

3. Use general education courses to sample possible majors. Your college has developed the general education requirements to provide you with the opportunity to become a well-rounded and well-informed person. Don't look at these as obligations, but as opportunities. From this variety, you may discover an interest you never knew you had.

4. For some majors, you have to begin early. Some majors have so many requirements that you must begin during your first semester in order to get everything in. Read the college catalog to see whether your major is one of those. The most common are such things as pre-engineering and fine arts (music).

5. If you have questions, ask an advisor. Some college seniors enjoy serving as advisors to freshmen, and some of their advice is valuable. But always check your questions about your degree program with a bona fide advisor. Don't feel like you are a pest.

If you have a question, go ask. That advisor is paid out of your tuition money. You are entitled to his time and knowledge.

6. Get everything in writing. This is repetition of a point made in the preceding chapter, but it is applicable here. Make sure you heard what the advisor said. Make him sign something.

7. When you do choose a major, remember that the primary purpose of a college education is to learn something.

16

Choosing a College

Test time! Since we are getting near the end of the book, we have come to the place for an exam. After all, the book is designed to prepare you for college life, and testing is a part of it.

People choose colleges based on one of two kinds of reasons—logical or illogical. Below is a list of the reasons students have given for choosing the college they attend. In the blank, at the left of each statement, write *L* if the statement if logical and *IL* if the statement is illogical.

_____ 1. This is where my parents went to school.

_____ 2. This is where my parents want me to go to school.

_____ 3. It is close to home.

_____ 4. It is a long way from home.

_____ 5. I like the climate.

_____ 6. It is what I can afford.

_____ 7. Good parties!

_____ 8. There is a good selection of the opposite sex.

_____ 9. This college offers the best education in the major I am pursuing.

_____10. It has a good academic reputation.

_____11. I like the social life here.

_____12. They offered me a scholarship.

_____13. I like the sports program (or music or drama).

_____14. I came to study with a specific professor.

_____15. My boyfriend or girl friend came.

_____16. Why did I come? I have wondered that myself.

_____17. The educational program will help me develop into a whole person.

_____18. I saw it advertised somewhere.

_____19. I heard it was easy and I want to pass.

_____20. I like what the college stands for.

_____21. This is where I was accepted.

_____22. The campus is pretty.

_____23. It is large enough to get lost in.

_____24. It is small enough for me to be known.

If this were a real test, I would provide you with a key so you could tell how many you answered correctly. But that wasn't my objective. Rather, I was simply trying to put you in touch with what you consider to be logical reasons for choosing a college. After all, you are the one who is going. You need to know what your interests and priorities are. You have to decide about what are valid and invalid reasons for your choice. In fact, I won't rebuke you if you choose a college for illogical reasons. It *is* your choice. You need to find someplace that matches your fingerprints.

If you have not yet chosen a college, you may want to go back through the list of reasons and label them as important or unimportant. This will help you develop criteria for measuring the various colleges you are considering. Thus, you can make the selection process systematic and scientific.

Other Considerations

Once you have determined your reasons for going to college and the conditions you are looking for in a college, there are a few pointers to consider as you confirm your choice.

1. Visit the school before you make the final decision. Don't rely completely on someone's report. Don't make the decision based on what the catalog and advertisements say. Go see for yourself. Just going to college and managing the social and academic demands is difficult enough at times. You don't need the added burden of going somewhere that doesn't meet your expectations.

If at all possible, make your visit a thorough one. Try to spend a few days. Live with another student in the dorm. Eat in the cafeteria. Go to class. If you have some idea of a major at this point, talk to the department head of that area. Gather as much information as you can.

Of course, this could be expensive in terms of both time and money, but going to a college you don't enjoy is even more expensive. Complete your research before you make a final decision.

2. Make sure you have an accurate appraisal of the academic quality. In other words, know what you are getting into. If you are going to a two-year college, make sure the credits can be transferred. If you are going to a four-year college to prepare for graduate school, find out the placement record.

Actually, there are two problems to consider here. The first is obvious when you think about it. Regardless of how good a college is, it is not equally good in everything. Some departments are better than others. For you, as a student in one particular area of study, the quality of a specific department helps determine the quality of the institution. The question to ask is the one listed in the chapter on choosing a major, "How is this department compared to the same department on other campuses?"

The second problem to consider is the kind of quality an institution has. There is a difference between real quality and perceived quality. Frequently, the two are the same, but this is not necessarily so. Some institutions are actually better than they look, while some are not as good as they first appear.

For example, a potential deceiver is the physical appearance of the campus itself. It is important for you to like the physical setting of the campus where you study; but the people you encounter, students and teachers, will always be more important to your surviving and thriving than the buildings and stadium.

Before you make your final decision, meet some of those people. See if you can be happy spending the next four years of your life with them. See if you can get along with them when the pressure builds and teardrops stain the pillowcase.

3. Once you have made your decision and have started, don't look back. One of the tricks to surviving and thriving in college is to adjust to whatever is happening. As long as you are still thinking, *I could have gone somewhere else,* you are just postponing adjustment. In fact, you are making things more difficult for yourself. Don't think those thoughts. Choose your college wisely. Make an intelligent decision; but once you have done that, be committed to making that decision work. Be committed to adjusting to where you are. There is no longer a known Garden of Eden on earth.

Each college has its unique advantages and problems. Your choice of a college is a matter of picking which set of advantages and problems best meet your personal, academic, and professional needs.

Choosing With a Base

One of the reasons I have placed this chapter on choosing a college so late in the book is that I wanted you to have all the other information about social and academic adjustment first. I want you to think about the kinds of people you will meet, the kinds of work you will do, the mindsets of the professors, your major, and the nature of institutions in general. A thorough knowledge of all this will contribute to your choosing the college just right for you—the one you will enjoy attending and the one you will enjoy talking about for the rest of your life. Of course, you realize that surviving and thriving in college is more than a four-year ordeal. It is a lifelong project. It is the remembering, the reunions, the football scores in Sunday's paper, the alumni magazine and activities, and the continuing correspondence with roommates and friends. Surely, you will keep this in mind when you make your choice.

17

Coming to the End

By now, you should be about ready to go to college. I hope that this book has given you some useful information, but I also hope it has done more than that. I hope that it has given you a sense of excitement about the whole college experience and a clearer vision of why you are going to college in the first place. College is more than a fun way to spend four years. It is the process of preparing for a fuller, happier, more rewarding life. But college is more than preparing for the future. It is a valuable experience within itself. I hope that you have realized that while reading this book.

Having some idea about how to manage the social relationships, handle the professors and classwork, and interact with the institution itself should give you something of a head start. That kind of knowledge could, in fact, make the whole experience easier and more fulfilling. At least, that was my intention in putting the information together. I wanted to relieve as much of your stress as I could so that you can relax and appreciate the significance of those four years.

Now that I have made some suggestions about how to go into the experience, I conclude the book by offering you some observations about how to come out of it. Too often, college freshmen tend to forget a very important point—some day college will be over. You need to get ready for that moment and for the life that comes after. In other words, you are also in the process of preparing for life after college.

I understand how difficult it is to think about the future, and I know how very difficult it is to think about the long-range future when the present and the immediate future offer so much excitement and change. But I would encourage you to give the long-range future at least a passing thought. Read this chapter now and catalog it in the back of your mind. You may want to dig it out to reread it during the last semester of your senior year, or you may want to pass it along to your senior friends who have suddenly realized that their immediate futures include leaving college. That can be a traumatic experience for anyone who has not thought about it before he gets there.

Structure

All your life up to the point when you leave college has had a definite direction, a purpose, a structure, a movement forward to a given point. That direction is there because of the nature of your goals, both short-term and long-range. Graduating from high school, graduating from college—those are definite, achievable objectives. At any given time, you can see where you are in relationship to the goal: how far you have come and how far you still must go. This ultimate goal provides structure for all areas of your life. On the route to the final goal there are thousands of immediate goals, deadlines, jobs, tasks, pressures—papers to write, chapters to read, people to see, problems to work, tests to take, pressures to live through—but you can see the purpose for each one of these because you know it relates to that one big goal—graduating from college.

With that goal in front of you, life has purpose. You have an instrument for measuring your own worth. Was last year a good year? Did I go anywhere? Did I make any progress? Did I do anything worthwhile? Yes, because I am now one year closer to my goal of graduating from college. Life has structure as well as purpose.

If you don't look ahead, college graduation can ruin all that. For most college graduates, life after college does not have that kind of structure, that kind of definite, achievable goal which the graduates can use as a measuring stick to determine the worth of their activities. Some of the more fortunate ones try to substitute other goals such as wealth, position, or power; but frequently they either don't achieve their goals or they don't find them as fulfilling as they thought they would be.

Others (myself included) play games. If you won't tell my publisher, I will let you in on a personal secret. This is one reason why I write books. I was a college student for a long time (the equivalent of nine years). In that time, I grew very dependent on those achievable goals to help me measure my self-worth and progress. When I finally won about as many degrees as I am capable of getting, I missed the definite goals in my life. I needed something out in front of me—a carrot on a stick—that let me know that I was getting somewhere, that every day had some significance because I was one day nearer my goal.

Writing books now serves that purpose. I now have something definite and long-range to shoot toward.

But I am one of the lucky ones. Thousands of my colleagues are still struggling for some kind of definition in life once that one objective of graduating from college is achieved.

I am not sure I know how to tell you to avoid this entirely, but I do want you to know of the possibility. Frequently, college seniors go through some rather painful moments when they suddenly realize that they are going to lose both the structure and the objective at graduation. Prepare yourself for that so you won't let the frustration throw you into unusual despair.

The Defense: Self-Concept

Perhaps the best defense against that possible frustration is to make sure that during your college experience you are building a good, strong self-concept. Of all the things you need to get out of college—a degree, friends, information, the ability to think and to evaluate thinking, perhaps even a spouse for life—the most important thing you need to get out of college is yourself. When the whole experience is over, you need to have a solid, objective view of yourself and a positive idea about what you are capable of doing in the world. Don't let the college experience rob you of this.

In the midst of all the frustrations, pressures, failures and near failures, embarrassments, successes, and appraisals of your own talent measured against talented people, don't forget that you are a unique human being with fingerprints unlike anyone else in the world. If the Creator put so much diligence into you that He drew a very special pattern just for you, then surely He made you something special.

The purpose of a college education is to provide the tools which allow you to develop that specialness. If you can keep that point firmly in mind, you should be able to survive and thrive through all the sorrows and joys in college—the heartaches and high spots, the tear-stained pillowcases and the uproarious hilarity of a well-performed practical joke. Once you have made it through college, you should be able to tackle the rest of your life with enthusiasm, intelligence, understanding, and commitment.

But on graduation day, when you make that transition from college life into what's after college, don't forget to come by and hug me. I want to celebrate with you.

Appendix

Financing Your College Education

If you have the desire to get a college degree and if you have the ability to do college work, you can get the money. In case you missed that, let me say it again. If you really want a college education and if you have the gumption to go to class, to meet your professors, to budget your time, and to study once in a while, you can get the money to pay for the venture from somewhere. Regardless of your family's financial situation, there is no need to deny yourself a college education because of the lack of funds. In fact, you may even be able to go to the college of your choice. Go ahead and check into it. You may be surprised. On graduation day, I have been hugged by young people from every economic bracket. Some of them once thought they could never get the money to go to *any* college, much less a private college such as ours.

If they can make it, so can you. You may not be able to operate a Ferrari or spend spring vacations in Fort Lauderdale, but you *can* afford to go to college. For one thing, there are several people pulling for you. If you are potentially a good student, the college itself wants you. Colleges are in business to educate students. If they don't have students, they go out of business. If you will be a good student and a good citizen, the college not only wants you, it *needs* you. The officials will work with you to try to get you into college.

Companies and corporations want you to go to college. These institutions fill their ranks with college graduates. If you don't go to college, they won't have anybody to hire. Thus, some company may offer you help.

And the government itself wants you to go to college, so state governments and the federal government offer a variety of programs to help you finance your college education.

Your task now is to find out where this money is and how you can get it. To help you get started, I give you the following information. However, I must remind you that this information is not complete. If you really want to go to college, do some research on your own. See your high school counselor or check with the college itself.

Financial Aid Officer

Begin here. When you narrow your choice of colleges down to a couple or so, check with the financial aid office to see what help is available and how you should apply. These people have the information. If you aren't satisfied, persist until you get all the data. But check with these people early in the procedure. Begin this process at least nine months before you will actually enroll.

Let me emphasize this point. Make no decisions until you have had a face-to-face discussion with the financial aid officer at the school you wish to attend. Don't be discouraged by newspaper articles and television reports that declare the high cost of college and the lack of funds available. Don't be alarmed by reports about cutbacks. You will never know whether you qualify for anything until you have checked. If you really want to go to college, there is a way to do it. Check with your high school counselor and get in touch with the college financial aid officer.

Financial Aid Forms

The majority of colleges use one of two standard forms for determining who qualifies for financial assistance. If you are going to try to get financial help for college expenses, you and your parents will have to fill out one of these. Which one you pick depends on the college. Check with the financial aid officer first. But be aware that this form must be completed and returned early in the enrollment procedure. Make sure you take care of this!

1. FAF or Financial Aid Form. This standard form is produced by the College Scholarship Service. Check with your high school counselor or the college financial aid officer for a form. You and your parents must fill it out and return it as directed.

2. FFS or Family Financial Statement. This standard form is produced by the American College Testing Company, the same company that handles some of the entrance exams. Again, check with your counselor or the college financial aid officer and have your parents complete it.

Scholarships

Scholarships are probably the best known source of college funds, but they may not necessarily be the best source for you. Scholarships come in several forms.

1. State Scholarships. Many states give scholarships to the students from their states. These are usually based on need (or your parents' ability to help you). Check with your high school counselor or college financial officer. Some states do require an application form other than the two mentioned earlier. This is a good source of funds for lower- and middle-income families.

2. Participation Scholarships. Sometimes the college pays a person to use his talents to help publicize the college. In other words, the college pays a person to play football, sing in the choir, or debate. The pay the talented person gets is called a participation scholarship. Unfortunately, this is probably the best known and most difficult scholarship to get and keep. If you are particularly talented in an area, you can write directly to the person who coaches or directs the activity in which you wish to participate.

3. Special Scholarships. There are literally thousands of specific scholarships to be awarded every year, and many of these go unclaimed simply because no one applies. However, many of these carry some unusual requirements, greatly limiting who can apply. As you are beginning to make your plans for college, check out all the possibilities. Many corporations and companies provide scholarships for the children of their employees. Have your parents check with their firms. Service clubs, churches, and special-interest groups also have scholarships. Check out all the possibilities where you or your parents have membership.

Colleges themselves frequently have special scholarships available to students in particular areas. Read that section of the college catalog to see whether you qualify for any of those.

Grants

A grant is a gift of money given by the federal government to students from low-income families. Although there have been some cutbacks here, money is still available. Don't be unduly alarmed by news reports. The college financial aid officer will know if you qualify after he has reviewed your financial aid form. Actually, these are called Pell Grants (formerly the Basic Educational Opportunity Grant). Since they are grants, they do not have to be repaid.

Loans

You may have to borrow a few dollars to get through college. So what else is new? If the desire and the ability are there, the experience is still worth the cost. There are at least two loan programs especially for college students. You may want to check into them.

1. Guaranteed Student Loan. These loans are issued by local banks, but they are guaranteed by the federal government. Since they are loans, you must pay back the money when you are finished with college. Check with your local banker.

2. National Direct Student Loans. In some cases, the federal government gives money directly to the college. Then, the financial aid officer is given the responsibility of lending it to the students who need it. Again, this is loan money. You must pay it back. Check with the college officer to see whether you qualify.

Service Contracts

Many young people, men and women alike, are getting some good college grants from the military branches. To receive financial help from a military branch (such as the Army or the Navy) the student must commit himself to participate in an officer's training program while he is in college. Then he must commit himself to a few years of active service following graduation. The student is still free to choose any major he wishes, and he is free to participate in all college activities. These scholarships from the military actually offer one advantage most scholarships don't offer—a guaranteed job after graduation.

Work

Another way to get the necessary money to finance your college education is the old-fashioned way—you can work for it. I am not really being facetious here. In fact, working at an outside job may be easier and less time-consuming than trying to keep some participation scholarships.

Colleges themselves often employ students for various positions around campus. Students often work as maintenance people, secretaries, library assistants, teaching assistants, and dorm counselors. Although the pay may not meet union scale, the hours are flexible enough to allow you to go to your classes and keep up with your study schedule.

In college towns, companies sometimes reserve certain positions for students. These may pay a bit better than the on-campus jobs, but they do create the problem of scheduling and transportation. To find one of these positions, you need to check with the employment office at the college. Remember! The college wants you to find a job so you can pay your bill. Check with the appropriate officer first.

Some college students find the work they need through service positions around the community. Many students have financed a big part of their college work through such jobs as house-cleaning, baby-sitting, tutoring, yard work, or house painting. If you are not afraid to work and if you are creative, there is an opportunity for you. One spring when I was in college, I started a lawn service business. I not only financed my education, I also put some money in the bank. (And I made the highest grades of my college career.)

I can summarize this chapter by reminding you of the beginning thesis. If you have the ability and the desire to go to college, *you can get the money.*

Glossary

Although most colleges have their own unique language and their own special names for almost everything around from courses to crabgrass, there are a few general terms which might help you as you make decisions among institutions, pick a major, plan your schedule, or conduct the business of getting admitted and paying for your first year. Even if you don't need all of these terms at your college, they will still help you understand some of the advice in this book.

College Officials

Admissions Director. The person who directs the process of deciding who gets admitted to a college. This person will have all the information about applications and testing. Contact him early in your decision-making process.

Advisor. Although there are several kinds of advisors, this term usually designates the person assigned to help you decide which classes to take and when to take them. Usually, your advisor will be a professor in the department of your major. You will need his signature on registration forms, drop and add slips, and special features of your program. Remember to get his suggestions in writing because your advisor may change during your four years.

Dean. Usually, this term designates the person who is in charge of something. There may be a dean of students, a dean of student services, a dean of academics, a dean of the college, a dean of the faculty, and so on. This means that this person is charged with taking care of this aspect of the college program. Some institutions may call these officers vice-presidents instead of deans.

Financial Aid Officer. The person who is in charge of handing out the scholarships and loans. You need to check with this person as soon as you decide which college you will be attending. He may have some money-saving suggestions for you.

Graduate Assistant. Universities that have graduate schools occasionally employ some select graduate students to teach some of the beginning courses in the department. Usually, these graduate assistants have been screened very carefully before they get such a position. Not only does the teaching assignment allow them to earn some of their tuition, but it also helps them learn more about the discipline they are studying. If you attend a university that employs graduate students for basic teaching assignments, you may have some as teachers for some of your freshmen courses.

President. This is the title usually given to the person who runs the place. In most colleges, this is the highest officer; however, some have a chancellor, who is something of a consultant to the president.

Professors. Of course, you know that a professor is the name used for a college teacher, but it may help you to know that professors come in different classes or ranks. Professors usually move up through the ranks according to the number of years they have been with the college and the quality of their work both in and out of the classroom (such as research, writing, and counseling). On rare occasions, the rank of the professor may have something to do with the quality of the course he teaches. However, rank is more important to professors than to students. The ranks are:

    1. *Instructors*—Usually, these are beginning teachers. Frequently, they have not yet earned a doctorate.

    2. *Assistant professors*—Usually, these are the relatively young Ph.D's who have been teaching for a short time.

3. *Associate professors*—These people are more established than those in the first two ranks. They have been around longer and perhaps have had some distinction in research or writing.

4. *Full professors or professors*—These are the veterans. They have probably taught for more than ten years, and they have done something significant to win the approval of the administration.

5. *Professor Emeritus*—A professor who retired after a rather long term of service.

Registrar. The person responsible for keeping the college records and making sure the academic rules are followed. If you need to see what courses will apply, how to get advanced credit, or what your grades are, you will go to the registrar's office. He also is responsible for sending out transcripts.

College Schedule

Hour. In college language, an hour is a unit of study. Courses are measured in hours; thus, your schedule and ultimately your degree is measured in hours. Usually, an hour means that the class meets one hour per week. In other words, a two-hour class meets two hours per week for the term, a three-hour class meets three hours per week, and so on. If you are taking sixteen hours during a given semester, that means you will go to class sixteen hours per week for that semester.

If you need 36 hours for a major, you will need nine 4-hour courses, twelve 3-hour courses, or some combination that totals 36 hours. If you need 124 hours to graduate, you will need some combination that totals 124 hours.

Semester. Colleges vary the length of their terms. Many use the semester. Usually, a semester is a sixteen-week term with classes meeting the first fifteen weeks and the final week reserved for final exams. If you go to a college with a semester calendar, your hours will be semester hours. There are two semesters during a nine-month period.

Trimester. Some colleges are using a term shorter than the traditional semester so that they can get three terms into a nine-month period. Thus, each term is called a trimester. Usually, this is between ten and eleven weeks long with some of the last week reserved for final exams. A trimester hour is roughly two-thirds of the value of a semester hour. In other words, if you need eighteen semester hours to qualify for a scholarship, you will need twenty-four trimester hours. The trimester schedule provides the student with a greater variety of courses.

Quarters. Some schools prefer to call their terms quarters. A quarter is approximately the same length as a trimester and the hour has similar value. Usually, schools that call these terms quarters put some emphasis on a summer term; thus, getting four terms per year.

4-1-4. Some schools, particularly smaller schools, are using some variation of the 4-1-4 calendar. In other words, they have two four-month (or fifteen-week) semesters, but they also have a short, one-month term in between. Frequently, this short term (minimester) is used for travel study or innovative courses on campus.

General Terms

General Education Requirements. Nearly every college requires each student to take some basic courses before graduation. Different names are used for these courses (sometimes the students give them unofficial names not suitable for printing), but frequently they are referred to as the general education requirements. Actually, the general education program has been constructed to help you get a basic understanding of all areas of the universe and academic world. You really should look forward to these. Usually, colleges that call themselves liberal arts colleges have more general education requirements than other schools.

Major. In nearly every college each student has to pick a course of study of major emphasis. In other words, he has to take more courses in this field than in any other. Thus, he *majors* in that field. The amount of hours he has to accumulate to complete a major is determined by the department he wishes to major in. The school catalog will provide that kind of information.

Minor. In some schools (particularly those that do not have a big general education requirement) students also need a minor. This is just another area of concentration but with fewer course requirements than a major.

Transcript. This is a record of your college grades. It is an important document which you will use frequently throughout your life. Your college will keep it on file for you; but when you need a copy, they will send it (for a fee, of course).

Entrance and Admissions Terms

Advance Deposit. After you have been admitted, the college may charge you an advance deposit. This is just to make you formally pledge to attend. If you are not going to enroll, the college can then give your spot to another applicant. If you do go, the advance deposit then goes into your account and will apply toward your bill.

Application Fee. This is a fee the college charges you for making an application to get in. Since the college has to supply the forms, and somebody has to make the effort of considering the application, the college wants you to be semiserious when you apply; thus, the fee. It is usually unrefundable, whether you get in or not.

College Boards. This is actually an organization of Educational Testing Service, a testing company in Princeton, New Jersey. The college board supervises a battery of three tests used by some colleges for entrance and placement in classes. These include:

    1. *SAT* (discussed later)

2. *Achievement tests*—Many colleges want you to take the college board Achievement Tests. They then use the scores to determine your ability in various fields and place you in classes where you will be both challenged and successful. There are a variety of these achievement tests, covering most of the subjects you studied in high school. Check with both your college admissions officer and your high school counselor to see which of these you should take.

3. *Advanced placements* (*AP*)—If your high school counselor and teachers think you qualify, the high school may give you permission to take the advanced placement portion of the college board tests. Many colleges will then give you college credit for those classes where you score high enough to meet the college standard. Thus, you may start college with some courses already on your transcript.

Testing. There are basically two major entrance examinations. Some colleges require one or the other; some will accept either, and some may require both. You need to check with the admissions director to find out for sure.

1. *ACT* (*American College Testing*)—The ACT reviews your ability in four areas—math, language, natural sciences, and social sciences. There is also a composite score. The national average is approximately 19. If your college wants the ACT score, check with your high school counselor.

2. *SAT* (*Scholastic Aptitude Test*)—This test measures your aptitude (or ability to perform) in two areas—math and verbal. The national average is approximately 897 total. If your college requires this, check with your counselor. (See College Boards above.)

3. *PSAT* (*Preliminary Scholastic Aptitude Test*)—This exam, usually given during the junior year in high school, helps you prepare for the SAT. The scores from the PSAT are used to determine the National Merit Scholarship competition.

NOTE: If a student is not satisifed with his scores on either the ACT or SAT he may retake the exam.